GREAT TASTES
DESSERTS

First published in 2009 by Bay Books, an imprint of Murdoch Books Pty Limited
This edition published in 2010.

Murdoch Books Australia
Pier 8/9
23 Hickson Road
Millers Point NSW 2000
Phone: +61 (0) 2 8220 2000
Fax: +61 (0) 2 8220 2558
www.murdochbooks.com.au

Murdoch Books UK Limited
Erico House, 6th Floor
93–99 Upper Richmond Road
Putney, London SW15 2TG
Phone: +44 (0) 20 8785 5995
Fax: +44 (0) 20 8785 5985
www.murdochbooks.co.uk

Chief Executive: Juliet Rogers
Publishing Director: Kay Scarlett
Publisher: Lynn Lewis
Senior Designer: Heather Menzies
Designer: Wendy Inkster
Production: Kita George
Index: Jo Rudd

ISBN: 9781741968712

PRINTED IN CHINA

IMPORTANT: Those who might be at risk from the effects of salmonella poisoning (the elderly, pregnant women, young children and those suffering from immune deficiency diseases) should consult their doctor with any concerns about eating raw eggs.

OVEN GUIDE: You may find cooking times vary depending on the oven you are using. For fan-forced ovens, as a general rule, set the oven temperature to 20°C (35°F) lower than indicated in the recipe.

GREAT TASTES

DESSERTS

More than 120 easy recipes for every day

bay books

CONTENTS

FRUIT

GRILLED MANGO CHEEKS WITH COCONUT ICE CREAM

SERVES 6

1 litre (35 fl oz/4 cups) vanilla ice cream, softened

30 g (1 oz/½ cup) shredded coconut, toasted

3 large ripe mangoes

2 tablespoons soft brown sugar

1 lime, halved

1 Mix the ice cream and coconut together in a large bowl, stirring only until just combined. Do not allow the ice cream to melt too much or it will become too icy. Return the mixture to the ice cream container and freeze for several hours, or overnight, until firm.

2 Preheat a barbecue flatplate, grill plate or chargrill pan to medium.

3 Cut 2 cheeks off each mango, so you have 6 cheeks. If you prefer to serve the mangoes without their skins, scoop the cheeks away from the skin using a large spoon, then sprinkle the cheeks with the sugar. Alternatively, leave the skin on and score the flesh in a criss-cross pattern, then sprinkle the flesh with sugar.

4 Put the mango cheeks flesh-side-down on the barbecue and grill for 1–2 minutes, or until the sugar has caramelized.

5 To serve, divide the cheeks among six serving bowls and drizzle with a squeeze of lime. Add a scoop or two of coconut ice cream.

Note: The coconut ice cream is delicious served with any fruit combination. Try pineapple and banana for a tropical flavour hit.

PEAR AND RASPBERRY CRUMBLE

SERVES 4

6 large pears (1.5 kg/3 lb 5 oz),
    ripe but firm

2 tablespoons caster (superfine) sugar

3 star anise

125 g (4½ oz/1 cup) raspberries

125 g (4½ oz/1 cup) plain
    (all-purpose) flour

95 g (3¼ oz/½ cup) soft brown sugar

100 g (3½ oz) unsalted butter,
    cut into cubes

ice cream, to serve

1 Preheat the oven to 190°C (375°F/Gas 5).

2 Peel, quarter and core the pears, then cut each piece in half lengthways.

3 Put into a large saucepan, and sprinkle the sugar over. Add 1 tablespoon of water and the star anise. Cover and bring to the boil.

4 Cook, covered, over medium–low heat for 10 minutes, stirring occasionally, until the fruit is tender but still holds its shape.

5 Drain the pears and discard the star anise, and transfer to a 1.5 litre (52 fl oz/6 cup) capacity ovenproof dish. Sprinkle the raspberries over the pears.

6 Combine the flour, sugar and butter in a bowl. Use your fingertips to rub the butter into the flour until the mixture resembles coarse breadcrumbs.

7 Sprinkle over the fruit, then bake for 20–25 minutes, until golden brown.

8 Stand for 5 minutes, then serve with ice cream.

SWEET DRUNKEN PINEAPPLE

SERVES 4

1 large pineapple or 2 small pineapples

oil, for brushing

40 g (1½ oz/¼ cup) coarsely grated palm sugar (jaggery) or soft brown sugar

2½ tablespoons rum

2 tablespoons lime juice

3 tablespoons small mint leaves

thick (double/heavy) cream, to serve

1 **Preheat a barbecue grill plate** or chargrill pan (griddle) to medium.

2 **Trim the ends from the pineapple,** remove the skin and cut into quarters lengthways.

3 **Brush the hot grill plate** or chargrill pan with oil, add the pineapple quarters and cook for about 10 minutes, turning to brown the cut sides.

4 **Take the pineapple** off the heat and cut each quarter into 1.5 cm (⅝ inch) thick slices. Overlap the slices on a large serving plate.

5 **Combine the sugar,** rum and lime juice in a small bowl, mixing well to dissolve the sugar. Pour the mixture evenly over the warm pineapple slices, then cover with plastic wrap and refrigerate for several hours.

6 **Serve at room temperature,** sprinkled with the mint leaves and a dollop of cream.

MIXED BERRY SUNDAE WITH RASPBERRY CREAM

SERVES 10

400 g (14 oz/1¾ cups) sugar

juice of 1 lemon

1 kg (2 lb 4 oz) mixed summer berries, including blueberries, loganberries, raspberries and strawberries

RASPBERRY CREAM

250 g (9 oz/2 cups) fresh raspberries

50 g (1¾ oz/½ cup) icing (confectioners') sugar

125 ml (4 fl oz/½ cup) thick (double/ heavy) cream

extra fresh berries, to serve

1 Put 500 ml (17 fl oz/2 cups) of water in a saucepan and add the sugar. Heat gently over low heat until the sugar has dissolved. Bring to the boil, then reduce the heat and simmer for 5 minutes. Set aside to cool, then stir in the lemon juice.

2 Put the sugar syrup and mixed berries in a large processor fitted with the metal blade and whizz for 20 seconds, or until smooth. Press the purée through a sieve in batches and pour into a wide, deep plastic container.

3 Freeze the mixture for 1–2 hours, or until ice crystals have formed around the edges.

4 Using an immersion blender or blender, whizz to break up the ice crystals. Return to the freezer and repeat this process for 4–5 hours until the berry mixture resembles soft snow.

5 To make the raspberry cream, whizz the raspberries and sugar in a small processor for 10 seconds, or until smooth. Press through a fine sieve. Lightly whip the cream until it just holds its shape. Fold the cream into the raspberry purée.

6 Serve the frozen sundae mixture in chilled glasses with a spoonful of raspberry cream and some fresh berries.

FIGS WITH AMARETTO MASCARPONE

SERVES 6

AMARETTO MASCARPONE

400 g (14 oz/2 cups) mascarpone
    cheese

2 tablespoons icing (confectioners')
    sugar

2 tablespoons amaretto liqueur

25 g (1 oz/¼ cup) ground almonds

1 tablespoon demerara or soft
    brown sugar

½ teaspoon ground cinnamon

9 fresh figs, halved

1 **To make the amaretto mascarpone,** thoroughly mix the mascarpone, icing sugar and amaretto in a bowl. Cover and refrigerate for 15 minutes, or until chilled.

2 **Heat the grill** (broiler) to high.

3 **In a small bowl,** combine the ground almonds, sugar and cinnamon.

4 **Sit the fig halves** on the grill tray and sprinkle with the almond mixture. Grill for about 4 minutes, or until the figs are hot, the sugar has melted and the tops are lightly browned.

5 **Serve hot,** dolloped with the chilled mascarpone, allowing 3 fig halves per person.

CARAMELIZED PEARS

SERVES 4

4 ripe corella pears, or other small sweet pears (see Note)
4 tablespoons demerara or soft brown sugar
40 g (1½ oz) butter, softened
1 tablespoon brandy
200 g (7 oz) crème fraîche, to serve
4 lemon wedges, to serve

1 Heat the grill (broiler) to high.

2 Peel the pears and halve them from top to bottom, keeping the stems intact if possible. Core the pears using a melon baller or a spoon.

3 Combine the sugar and butter in a small bowl, then stir in the brandy.

4 Sit the pears, cut-side-down, on the grill tray, and brush the tops with some of the sugar mixture. Grill for about 5 minutes, or until lightly browned.

5 Turn the pears, brush with a little more sugar mixture, then fill the cavities with the remaining mixture. Grill for a further 3 minutes, or until the sugar is bubbling and golden brown. Baste again, then grill for a further 3 minutes.

6 Remove from the heat and leave the pears for 5 minutes, then serve with a scoop of crème fraîche, a squeeze of lemon juice and any juices from the grill tray.

Note: If you are unable to obtain small pears, you could use 4 larger pears and increase the cooking time slightly.

BAKED ALMOND AND MARZIPAN PEACHES

SERVES 6

3 large ripe firm peaches

40g (1½ oz/⅓ cup) roughly chopped dark chocolate

50g (1¾ oz/⅓ cup) whole blanched almonds, toasted and chopped

2½ tablespoons marzipan, chopped

2 tablespoons caster (superfine) sugar

1½ tablespoons unsalted butter, softened

1 egg yolk, lightly beaten

thick (double/heavy) cream or crème anglaise, to serve (see page 51)

2 tablespoons soft brown sugar

1 **Preheat the oven** to 170°C (325°F/Gas 3). Lightly grease a roasting tin or large ceramic ovenproof dish.

2 **Cut the peaches** in half on either side of the stone. Remove any remaining flesh from the stone and finely chop, then place in a bowl with the remaining ingredients, stirring to combine.

3 **Place the peaches**, skin side down, in the tin. Divide the stuffing mixture among the peaches, pressing it firmly onto each one and heaping the mixture slightly if necessary. Bake for 30 minutes, or until the peaches have softened and the filling is bubbling.

4 **Cool slightly,** then serve warm or at room temperature with thick cream or crème anglaise.

BRIOCHE WITH BANANAS AND MAPLE SYRUP

SERVES 4

4 sugar or finger bananas

2 tablespoons soft brown sugar

25 g (1 oz) butter, melted

1 tablespoon orange juice

2 eggs

125 ml (4 fl oz/½ cup) milk

185 ml (6 fl oz/¾ cup) maple syrup

4 thick slices brioche

icing (confectioners') sugar, for dusting

fresh blueberries, to serve

1 Preheat a barbecue grill plate or flat plate to medium.

2 Peel the bananas and cut them in half lengthways.

3 Put the sugar, butter and orange juice in a small bowl and mix well until the sugar has dissolved. Brush the mixture evenly over the bananas on all sides.

4 In a bowl, whisk the eggs and milk together with 2 tablespoons of the maple syrup. Dip the brioche slices in the mixture, coating well on both sides.

5 Lightly brush the barbecue grill plate or flat plate with oil and cook the bananas and brioche for 2–3 minutes, or until the bananas are tender and both the brioche and bananas are nicely browned.

6 Divide the brioche among four serving bowls or plates. Sprinkle with blueberries, then arrange 2 banana halves on top. Drizzle with the remaining maple syrup, dust lightly with icing sugar and serve.

APRICOT AND COCONUT FOOL

SERVES 4

20 g (¾ oz/⅓ cup) shredded coconut

300 ml (10½ fl oz) thick (double/heavy) cream

30 g (1 oz/¼ cup) icing (confectioners') sugar

15 tinned apricot halves, drained

1 teaspoon natural vanilla extract

1 Preheat the grill (broiler) to medium–high.

2 Spread the shredded coconut on a baking sheet. Place 12 cm (5 inches) below the heat and toast, stirring once or twice, for about 3 minutes, or until just starting to brown.

3 Put the cream and 1 tablespoon of the sugar in a large processor fitted with the whisk attachment and whisk until medium peaks form (or, use electric beaters). Spoon into a large bowl.

4 Change the blade on the processor to the metal blade and add the apricot halves, vanilla and the remaining sugar. Whizz for 15 seconds, or until puréed.

5 Roughly fold the apricot mixture into the cream; do not completely combine, but leave ripples of the apricot running through the cream.

6 Spoon into four glass bowls, sprinkle with the toasted coconut and serve.

PASSIONFRUIT CREAM WITH SNAP BISCUITS

SERVES 6–8

SNAP BISCUITS

100 g (3½ oz/⅔ cup) blanched almonds

115 g (4 oz/½ cup) caster (superfine) sugar

60 g (2¼ oz) unsalted butter, softened

1 tablespoon plain (all-purpose) flour

1 egg white

8 passionfruit

125 g (4½ oz/1 cup) raspberries

250 g (9 oz/1 cup) ricotta cheese

50 g (1¾ oz/½ cup) icing (confectioners') sugar, sifted, plus extra for dusting

½ teaspoon natural vanilla extract

150 ml (5 fl oz) thick (double/heavy) cream, whipped

icing (confectioners') sugar, for dusting

1 To make the snap biscuits, preheat the oven to 180°C (350°F/Gas 4). Line two baking sheets with baking paper.

2 Put the almonds and half the caster sugar in a small processor fitted with the metal blade and whizz for 1 minute, or until a fine powder forms. Add the remaining sugar, the butter, flour and egg white and whizz until just combined.

3 Drop rounded teaspoons of mixture 5 cm (2 inches) apart onto one of the prepared baking sheets and flatten them with the back of a spoon. Bake for 7–8 minutes, or until golden. Remove from the oven and slide the paper with the biscuits onto a flat surface to cool. Repeat with the remaining mixture.

4 Halve six of the passionfruit and strain the juice through a fine sieve into a bowl. Discard the pulp. Halve the remaining passionfruit, scoop the pulp into a bowl and gently stir in the raspberries, reserving a few raspberries for garnishing. Cover and chill until needed.

5 Put the ricotta, icing sugar, vanilla and strained passionfruit juice into the clean processor fitted with the plastic blade. Whizz for 30 seconds, then scrape down the side of the bowl. Repeat until the mixture is smooth, then transfer to a large bowl. Using a metal spoon, carefully fold the whipped cream through the ricotta mixture until well combined. Cover and refrigerate until needed.

6 To serve, gently fold the raspberry mixture through the passionfruit cream. Put one of the snap biscuits on each plate, spoon on the passionfruit cream, then top with another biscuit. Dust with icing sugar and garnish with the reserved raspberries. Serve immediately.

ORANGES IN SPICED SYRUP

SERVES 4

4 oranges, peeled and sliced widthways into 1 cm (½ inch) thick slices

185 g (6½ oz/¾ cup) Greek-style yoghurt

3 tablespoons thick (double/heavy) cream

1 teaspoon honey

SYRUP

115 g (4 oz/½ cup) grated palm sugar (jaggery) or soft brown sugar

1 star anise

2 vanilla beans, split, seeds scraped

1 cinnamon stick

1 tablespoon orange flower water (see Note)

zest of 1 orange, peeled in thick strips

1 Arrange the orange slices on a plate that fits into a large steamer, then put the plate in the steamer and cover with a lid. Sit the steamer over a saucepan or wok of boiling water and steam for 5–8 minutes, or until the oranges are warm and have started to release some of their juices. Carefully remove the plate from the steamer. Using a spatula, lift the orange slices into a bowl and reserve the orange liquid.

2 To make the syrup, put the sugar and 185 ml (6 fl oz/ ¾ cup) of water in a small saucepan over medium–high heat and stir until the sugar has dissolved. Add the star anise, vanilla beans and seeds, cinnamon stick, orange flower water, orange zest and reserved orange liquid and simmer for 10 minutes, or until the liquid has reduced by half. Pour the syrup over the oranges and leave to cool completely. Refrigerate for 1 hour to chill well.

3 When you are ready to serve, combine the yoghurt, cream and honey. Put three or four slices of orange on individual serving plates and top with a vanilla bean half and some orange zest. Drizzle with a little of the syrup and serve with a generous dollop of honey yoghurt.

Note: Orange flower water is a popular ingredient in Middle Eastern desserts. It is available from health food shops and delicatessens, and can sometimes be found in the cake-making section of larger supermarkets.

BANANA AND PLUM CRUMBLE

SERVES 4–6

30 g (1 oz/¼ cup) plain (all-purpose) flour

50 g (1¾ oz/½ cup) rolled oats

30 g (1 oz/½ cup) shredded coconut

45 g (1¾ oz/¼ cup) lightly packed soft brown sugar

finely grated zest from 1 lime

100 g (3½ oz) unsalted butter, cut into cubes

2 bananas, peeled and halved lengthways

4 plums, halved and stoned

60 ml (2 fl oz/¼ cup) lime juice

1 **Preheat the oven** to 180°C (350°F/Gas 4).

2 **Combine the flour,** rolled oats, coconut, sugar and zest in a small bowl. Add the butter and, using your fingertips, rub the butter into the flour mixture until crumbly.

3 **Put the bananas and plums** in a 1.25 litre (44 fl oz/5 cup) capacity ovenproof dish and pour over the lime juice. Toss to coat in the juice.

4 **Sprinkle the crumble mixture** evenly over the fruit. Bake for 25–30 minutes, or until the crumble is golden.

5 **Serve hot** with ice cream or whipped cream.

WAFFLES TOPPED WITH SOFT MERINGUE AND SAUCE

SERVES 4

LIME AND RASPBERRY SAUCE
150 g (5½ oz/1¼ cups) raspberries
1 tablespoon caster (superfine) sugar
1 teaspoon finely grated lime zest

4 ready-made waffles
2 egg whites
80 g (2¾ oz/⅓ cup) caster
   (superfine) sugar

1 **To make the lime** and raspberry sauce, put the raspberries in a small saucepan with the sugar, lime zest and 2 tablespoons water. Simmer over low heat for about 3 minutes, stirring gently until the sugar has dissolved, taking care not to break up the raspberries. Set aside, but keep warm.

2 **Heat the grill** (broiler) to low. Put the waffles on the grill tray and grill for 30 seconds on each side, or until golden. Remove from the grill tray, but leave the grill on.

3 **Beat the egg** whites in a small bowl using electric beaters until soft peaks form. Slowly add sugar 1 tablespoon at a time, beating well after each addition, and scraping the sides of the bowl with a spatula between beatings. Continue beating until the meringue becomes thick and glossy — this will take about 3 minutes.

4 **Using a large spoon** or spatula, spread the meringue evenly all over each waffle, ensuring the entire surface is thickly covered. Gently swirl the meringue into little peaks, using the tip of your spoon or spatula.

5 **Sit the waffles** on the grill tray and grill for 3–5 minutes, or until the meringue peaks turn golden brown — watch them carefully to ensure they don't burn.

6 **Serve the waffles warm,** drizzled with the lime and raspberry sauce.

BAKED PEARS IN SPICED SAUTERNES SYRUP

SERVES 6

250 ml (9 fl oz/1 cup) Sauternes or any dessert wine

345 g (12 oz/1½ cups) caster (superfine) sugar

2 cardamom pods, bruised

2 cloves

1 cinnamon stick

1 star anise

1 teaspoon rosewater

1 small piece of lemon rind, white pith removed

6 corella (or other small) pears, peeled

125 g (4½ oz/½ cup) Greek-style yoghurt, to serve

1 tablespoon honey, to serve

1 **Preheat the oven** to 180°C (350°F/Gas 4).

2 **Combine** 750 ml (26 fl oz/3 cups) water with the Sauternes, sugar, cardamom, cloves, cinnamon, star anise, rosewater and lemon rind in a saucepan. Stir over medium heat for 4–5 minutes, or until the sugar dissolves. Bring the mixture to the boil, then reduce the heat to low and cook for 8 minutes, or until the syrup has reduced by half.

3 **Halve the pears,** place them in a roasting tin and pour over the syrup. Cover with foil and bake for 20 minutes. Remove the foil, baste the pears with the syrup, then cook for a further 20 minutes, or until the pears are tender.

4 **Serve the pears warm** or at room temperature with the yoghurt and a little honey spooned over.

SPICED CARAMELIZED BANANAS

SERVES 4

50 g (1¾ oz) unsalted butter

2 tablespoons soft brown sugar

½ teaspoon ground nutmeg

¼ teaspoon ground allspice

4 bananas, peeled and sliced lengthways

grated zest and juice of 1 orange

1 tablespoon rum

2 tablespoons lightly roasted pecans or walnuts, chopped

freshly grated nutmeg, to sprinkle

ice cream, to serve

1 **Put the butter,** sugar, nutmeg and allspice in a frying pan over medium heat. Mix until combined and cook for 1 minute, or until the sugar has dissolved.

2 **Add the bananas,** cut side down, and cook for 2 minutes, or until a little softened. Remove the bananas and transfer to a serving plate.

3 **Add the orange zest** and juice to the frying pan and stir for 2 minutes, or until mixture thickens and is syrupy. Stir in the rum. Spoon the sauce over the bananas. Sprinkle with the chopped nuts and sprinkle with some freshly grated nutmeg.

4 **Serve warm** with scoops of vanilla ice cream.

SWEET BRUSCHETTA

SERVES 4

250 g (9 oz/1½ cups) strawberries

200 g (7 oz/1¾ cups) ricotta cheese

1 tablespoon icing (confectioners') sugar, plus extra to serve

2 teaspoons Grand Marnier, or other orange-flavoured liqueur

30 g (1 oz/¼ cup) toasted slivered almonds

4 thick slices panettone, brioche or other sweet bread

2 tablespoons soft brown sugar

1 Heat the grill (broiler) to high.

2 Reserve 4 small strawberries and chop the rest into 5 mm (¼ inch) cubes. Put them in a bowl with the ricotta, icing sugar, Grand Marnier and almonds, and gently mix together.

3 Put the bread slices on the grill tray and grill for about 1 minute, or until golden brown on top.

4 Turn the slices over, spread the ricotta mixture over the top and sprinkle with the sugar. Grill for about 45 seconds, or until the sugar has melted and the surface bubbles and browns.

5 Transfer to a serving plate and dust lightly with icing sugar. Place a reserved strawberry on each slice and serve hot.

ROASTED SPICED PEARS AND STRAWBERRIES

SERVES 4

170 g (6 oz/¾ cup) caster (superfine)
   sugar

2 vanilla beans, split lengthways

2 star anise

1 cinnamon stick, broken in half

4 firm pears, peeled and cut into
   quarters

250 g (9 oz/1⅔ cups) strawberries,
   hulled, cut in half if large

Greek-style yoghurt, to serve

1 Preheat the oven to 170°C (325°F/Gas 3).

2 Put 310 ml (10¾ fl oz/1¼ cups) of water, and the sugar,
vanilla beans, star anise and cinnamon in an ovenproof dish.
Place in the oven and cook for 10 minutes, stirring once, until
the sugar dissolves.

3 Add the pears to the syrup. Cover with foil and cook
for 35–45 minutes, or until almost tender, turning once in
the syrup.

4 Add the strawberries and turn to coat in the syrup.
Cover with foil and cook for a further 5 minutes, or until the
strawberries soften.

5 Set aside to cool to room temperature and serve
with yoghurt.

NECTARINE AND FIG KEBABS WITH ROSEWATER SYRUP

SERVES 4

ROSEWATER SYRUP

230 g (8 oz/1 cup) caster (superfine) sugar

2 teaspoons rosewater

1 tablespoon lemon juice

8 nectarines, cut in half, stones removed

8 fresh figs, cut in half

125 g (4½ oz/½ cup) thick plain yoghurt

2 tablespoons honey

2 tablespoons chopped pistachio nuts

1   **To make the rosewater syrup,** put the sugar in a saucepan with 250 ml (9 fl oz/1 cup) water. Stir, bring to the boil, then reduce the heat and simmer for 10 minutes. Remove from the heat and stir in the rosewater and lemon juice.

2   **Soak eight** bamboo skewers in cold water for 30 minutes. Thread a skewer through the side of a nectarine half, then a fig half, then another nectarine half and another fig half. Repeat to make 8 fruit kebabs. Put them in a large, flat non-metallic dish, then pour on the rosewater syrup. Cover and refrigerate for up to 3 hours.

3   **Heat a barbecue flat plate** to high and lightly brush with oil. When the plate is hot, cook the kebabs for 5 minutes, turning once, and brushing with a little more rosewater syrup during cooking.

4   **Put 2 kebabs** on each serving plate, drizzle with the yoghurt and honey, sprinkle with the pistachios and serve.

BANANA AND PEAR PARCELS WITH PASSIONFRUIT SAUCE

SERVES 4

20 g (¾ oz) butter

2 tablespoons maple syrup

4 bananas, cut into large chunks

3 ripe pears, peeled, quartered
  and cored

PASSIONFRUIT SAUCE

pulp of 4 large passionfruit

2 tablespoons soft brown sugar

vanilla ice cream, to serve (optional)

1   Preheat the oven to 180°C (350°F/Gas 4). Cut out four 30 cm (12 inch) squares of baking paper.

2   Melt the butter and maple syrup in a small saucepan over low heat. Divide the banana chunks and pear quarters among the paper squares, then spoon the maple butter mixture over the top.

3   For each parcel, bring two paper edges up to the centre and pleat. Pleat the sides to form a secure parcel. Put the parcels on a baking tray and bake for 10 minutes, or until the bananas are softened but still firm.

4   Meanwhile, to make the passionfruit sauce, combine the passionfruit pulp and sugar and stir until dissolved.

5   To serve, remove the fruit and sauce from the paper cases and arrange on serving plates. Drizzle with the sauce and serve with a scoop of ice cream, if desired.

PEARS WITH ROSE JELLY AND CITRUS SYRUP

SERVES 6

ROSE JELLY (GELATIN DESSERT)

600 ml (21 fl oz) rosé wine

225 g (8 oz/1 cup) caster (superfine) sugar

2½ tablespoons powdered gelatine

6 small pears

1 star anise

1 cinnamon stick

8 cardamom pods

8 whole cloves

CITRUS SYRUP

225 g (8 oz/1 cup) caster (superfine) sugar

1 teaspoon grated lime zest

1 tablespoon lime juice

1 teaspoon grated orange zest

1 tablespoon orange juice

1 To make the rosé jelly, pour the wine into a saucepan and bring to the boil. Remove the pan from the heat and stir in the sugar until it has dissolved. Put the gelatine in a glass bowl, pour in 250 ml (9 fl oz/1 cup) of the heated wine, and stir briskly with a fork until dissolved. Stir in the remaining wine, then pour into six 125 ml (4 fl oz/½ cup) moulds. Allow to cool, then refrigerate for 3–4 hours, or until set.

2 Peel and core the pears, leaving the stem on. Cut across the bottom of each pear so they stand up in the steamer.

3 Half-fill a saucepan or wok with water and add the star anise, cinnamon, cardamom and cloves. Bring the water to the boil, then reduce the heat and keep at a rapid simmer.

4 Stand the pears in a steamer in a single layer and cover with a lid. Sit the steamer over the saucepan and steam for 15 minutes, or until a skewer can be inserted with ease all the way through.

5 Meanwhile, to make the syrup, combine the sugar and 250 ml (9 fl oz/1 cup) of water in a small saucepan and stir over low heat until the sugar has dissolved. Add the citrus zests and juices, bring to the boil, then reduce the heat and simmer without stirring for 10–15 minutes. Take the pan off the heat. Remove the pears from the steamer and put them in the warm citrus syrup while plating up the jelly.

6 To serve, dip the moulds in hot water for a few seconds. Place a plate on top and turn out the jelly. Serve immediately with the steamed pears and a generous drizzle of citrus syrup.

WARM DRIED FRUIT SALAD WITH HONEY YOGHURT

SERVES 4

400 g (14 oz) assorted dried fruit,
  such as prunes, apples, apricots
  and pears

1 cinnamon stick, broken in half

30 g (1 oz/⅓ cup) flaked almonds,
  toasted

HONEY YOGHURT

200 g (7 oz/heaped ¾ cup)
  Greek-style yoghurt

2 tablespoons honey

2 teaspoons rosewater

1 Put the dried fruit and cinnamon stick on a plate large enough to just fit into a large steamer. Put the plate in the steamer and cover with a lid. Sit the steamer over a saucepan or wok of boiling water and steam for 20–25 minutes, or until the fruit is plump.

2 To make the honey yoghurt, combine the yoghurt, honey and rosewater in a bowl.

3 To serve, divide the fruit among four serving bowls and scatter the almonds over the top. Serve with the honey yoghurt.

STICKY RICE WITH MANGO

SERVES 4

400 g (14 oz/2 cups) glutinous white rice (see Note)
250 ml (9 fl oz/1 cup) coconut milk
60 g (2¼ oz/⅓ cup) grated palm sugar (jaggery) or soft brown sugar
4 kaffir lime leaves, crushed
1 lemongrass stem, bruised
2 mangoes
2 teaspoons grated palm sugar or soft brown sugar, extra
1 lime, quartered

1 **Wash the rice** under cold running water until the water runs clear. Put it in a bowl, cover with cold water and leave overnight. Drain.

2 **Line a large steamer** with baking paper and punch with holes. Put the rice on top and cover with a lid. Sit the steamer over a wok or saucepan of boiling water and steam until the rice is soft (this will take 30–60 minutes, depending on the size of your steamer).

3 **Meanwhile,** put the coconut milk, palm sugar, lime leaves and lemongrass in a small saucepan and stir over low heat until the sugar has dissolved. Bring to a simmer and cook for 5 minutes, or until thickened.

4 **Transfer the soft rice** to a large bowl and pour the coconut mixture over the top, fluffing the rice with a fork as you pour to coat the rice evenly. Do not stir or the rice will become gluggy. Cover and leave for 10 minutes to absorb the liquid, then remove the lemon grass and lime leaves.

5 **Cut the cheeks** from the mangoes to give four cheeks. Cut through the mango flesh in a lattice pattern, taking care not to cut through the skin, and push the skin up to expose the flesh. Sprinkle with the extra palm sugar and serve with the sticky rice and a wedge of lime.

Note: Glutinous rice is also known as sticky rice and is used in both sweet and savoury Asian dishes. It needs overnight soaking prior to cooking. If you don't have time, you can soak the rice for half the time but you will need to increase the cooking time by up to 30 minutes.

BANANA SOY MILK PANCAKES WITH HONEYCOMB BUTTER

SERVES 4

HONEYCOMB BUTTER

60 g (2¼ oz) butter, softened

1 tablespoon honey

50 g crushed honeycomb

PANCAKES

2 bananas

325–375 ml (11–13 fl oz) vanilla soy milk

2 eggs

1 tablespoon caster (superfine) sugar

30 g (1 oz) butter, melted

1 teaspoon natural vanilla extract

185 g (6½ oz/1½ cups) self-raising flour

½ teaspoon bicarbonate of soda
    (baking soda)

icing (confectioners') sugar, to serve

ice cream, to serve

1 To make the honeycomb butter, beat the butter and honey together, then fold through the crushed honeycomb.

2 To make the pancakes, cut one of the bananas into pieces and put in a blender. Add three-quarters of the soy milk, the eggs, sugar, melted butter and the vanilla. Whizz for 10–15 seconds, or until the batter is smooth. Add the remaining soy milk a little at a time. Add the flour and bicarbonate of soda and whizz in short bursts for 30 seconds, or until the mixture is well combined and smooth. Pour the batter into a pitcher.

3 Thinly slice the remaining banana and stir it into the batter.

4 Heat a large non-stick frying pan over medium heat and lightly grease with melted butter. Pour 60 ml (2 fl oz/¼ cup) of the batter into the pan and cook for 2 minutes, or until bubbles appear on the surface. Turn and cook for 2 minutes or until cooked and golden. Transfer the pancake to a wire rack and cover with a tea towel (dish towel) to keep warm while you cook the remaining pancakes.

5 Serve the pancakes dusted with icing sugar and topped with a small scoop of ice cream and the honeycomb butter.

PEAR AND GINGER FILO PARCELS

SERVES 4

30 g (1 oz/¼ cup) small seedless raisins or sultanas

1 tablespoon cognac or pear eau-de-vie

2 teaspoons lemon juice

3 Bosc pears

50 g (1¾ oz) ginger nut biscuits (ginger snaps), roughly broken

40 g (1½ oz/¼ cup) soft brown sugar

½ teaspoon mixed (pumpkin pie) spice

2 tablespoons cornflour (cornstarch)

1 egg yolk

8 sheets filo pastry

canola oil spray

icing (confectioners') sugar, to serve

softened vanilla ice cream, to serve

1   Preheat the oven to 190°C (375°F/Gas 5). Line a baking tray with baking paper.

2   Put the raisins and liqueur in a small bowl and set aside.

3   Put the lemon juice in a bowl. Peel, quarter and core the pears. Add them to the bowl and toss to coat with the lemon juice.

4   Put the ginger nut biscuits in a mini processor and add the sugar, mixed spice and cornflour. Whizz for 15 seconds, or until the mixture forms fine crumbs. Roughly chop half the pears and add to the processor. Add the egg yolk and whizz in two-second bursts for 15–25 seconds, or until the pears are chopped medium–fine. The mixture will be quite thin.

5   Cut the remaining pears into 2 cm (¾ inch) dice and return to their bowl. Add the raisin mixture and processed pear mixture and toss to combine.

6   Lay a sheet of filo on a work surface and spray with oil. Fold in half, one short side over the other and spray with oil. Top with another sheet of filo, fold that in half and spray with oil, giving four layers of pastry. Trim the pastry to an 18 cm (7 inch) square. Spoon one-quarter of the pear filling onto the centre. Starting at one corner, fold the filo over the filling to make a fat, square envelope. Ensure that the filling is well contained, and spray dry surfaces of the pastry as you fold. Spray the parcel all over with oil and place on the prepared tray, fold side up. Make three more parcels using the rest of the pastry and filling.

7   Bake for 20-25 minutes, or until the parcels are crisp and golden.

8   Serve hot, dusted with icing sugar and with a little softened vanilla ice cream spooned on top.

NECTARINE CRUMBLE WITH MAPLE AND LIME SYRUP

SERVES 4

3 tablespoons maple syrup

1 teaspoon finely grated lime zest

4 ripe nectarines, cut in half, stones removed

30 g (1 oz/¼ cup) self-raising flour

30 g (1 oz) unsalted butter, chilled and chopped

2 tablespoons soft brown sugar

1 Put the maple syrup and lime zest in a bowl. Stir well and leave to infuse for 15 minutes.

2 Heat the grill (broiler) to medium.

3 Lightly brush the cut side of the nectarine halves with some of the syrup. Put the nectarine halves, cut side down, in a lightly oiled non-stick frying pan. Gently fry over low–medium heat for 1 minute on each side, or until slightly soft.

4 Put the flour in a small bowl and add the butter. Using your fingertips, rub the butter into the flour until the mixture resembles breadcrumbs, then stir through the sugar.

5 Place the nectarines on the grill tray, cut side up. Lightly brush them with a little more syrup, then sprinkle crumble mixture over the top. Grill for 2 minutes, or until the crumble turns golden brown.

6 To serve, divide among four serving bowls and drizzle with the remaining syrup. This dessert is delicious served with vanilla ice cream.

CREPES WITH RICOTTA AND SOUR CHERRIES

SERVES 4

CREPE BATTER

90 g (3¼ oz/¾ cup) plain (all-purpose) flour

2 eggs

20 g (¾ oz) butter, melted

310 ml (11 fl oz/1¼ cups) milk

RICOTTA FILLING

375 g (13 oz/1½ cups) fresh ricotta cheese

80 g (2¾ oz/⅓ cup) caster (superfine) sugar

½ teaspoon finely grated orange zest

80 g (2¾ oz) crème fraîche

½ teaspoon vanilla extract

30 g (1 oz) butter, softened

80 g (2¾ oz/⅓ cup) semi-dried (sun-blushed) sour cherries (see Note)

TOPPING

2 eggs

3 tablespoons caster (superfine) sugar

125 ml (4 fl oz/½ cup) thick (double/heavy) cream, lightly whipped

2 teaspoons orange-flavoured liqueur, such as Cointreau

icing (confectioners') sugar, for dusting

1 **To make the crepe batter,** sift the flour into a large bowl and make a well in the centre. In a separate bowl, mix together the eggs, butter and milk. Gradually whisk the milk mixture into the flour, beating well to make a smooth, lump-free batter. Strain to remove any lumps if necessary, then leave to stand for 10 minutes. Transfer to a jug for easier pouring.

2 **While the batter** is resting, make the ricotta filling. Put the ricotta, sugar, orange zest, crème fraîche, vanilla and butter in a bowl and mix until smooth. Stir in the cherries.

3 **Heat the grill** (broiler) to medium. Put a lightly greased 26 cm (10½ inch) non-stick frying pan over medium heat. When the pan is hot, pour in a small amount of batter and swirl to thinly coat the base. Cook for 1–2 minutes, or until lightly browned, then flip the crepe over and brown the other side. Repeat with the remaining mixture to make 8 crepes.

4 **Lay the crepes** on a work surface. Divide the filling evenly among them, placing it along the bottom edge in a narrow log and leaving a margin at each side of the filling. Gently roll up the crepes, tucking the sides in as you go. Put the crepes in a large, shallow ovenproof dish or four individual ovenproof dishes and grill for about 5 minutes, or until warmed through.

5 **While the crepes are grilling,** make the topping. Using an electric mixer, beat the eggs and sugar in a small bowl until light and fluffy. Fold in the cream and liqueur. Spoon the mixture over the warmed crepes, then return them to the grill and cook for about 5 minutes, or until golden brown. Serve with a dusting of icing sugar.

Note: Semi-dried sour cherries are often available at speciality food stores.

TROPICAL ETON MESS

SERVES 4

MERINGUES

1 egg white, at room temperature

55 g (2 oz/¼ cup) caster (superfine) sugar

FILLING

125 g (4½ oz/heaped ¾ cup) strawberries, thickly sliced

½ small red papaya, seeded, peeled and cubed

pulp of 4 passionfruit

1 tablespoon caster (superfine) sugar

1 tablespoon raspberry liqueur, such as Framboise, or orange liqueur, such as Grand Marnier (optional)

TOPPING

170 ml (5½ fl oz/⅔ cup) thick (double/heavy) cream

175 g (6 oz/scant ¾ cup) Greek-style yoghurt

1 To make the meringues, preheat the oven to 130°C (250°F/Gas 1) and line a baking tray with baking paper. Beat the egg white until stiff peaks form. Add 1 tablespoon of the caster sugar and beat for 3 minutes, or until glossy. Add another tablespoon of sugar and beat for another 3 minutes. Add the remaining sugar and the cornflour and beat for 2 minutes.

2 Put four even-sized heaped spoonfuls of the meringue mixture on the prepared tray. Bake for 30 minutes, or until the meringues are firm on the outside. Turn off the oven and leave them in the oven until the oven is cold. Roughly crumble the meringues.

3 Combine the strawberries, papaya and half the passionfruit pulp in a bowl. Stir in the sugar and the liqueur, if using. Set aside for 5 minutes, or until ready to assemble.

4 Just before serving, beat the cream in a bowl until thick. Stir in the yoghurt. Add the fruit mixture all at once and stir until roughly combined.

5 To serve, spoon half the mixture into 4 x 310 ml (10¾ fl oz/1¼ cup) tall parfait glasses. Top with the crumbled meringue and then the remaining fruit. Garnish with the remaining passionfruit pulp and serve immediately.

Note: Eton Mess was traditionally served at Eton College, in England, at prize-giving day. The term 'mess' may refer to the dessert's appearance.

POACHED VANILLA PEACHES WITH RASPBERRY PUREE

SERVES 4

350 g (12 oz/1½ cups) caster (superfine) sugar

1 vanilla bean, halved lengthways

4 peaches

100 g (3½ oz/heaped ¾ cup) fresh raspberries or frozen raspberries, thawed

4 small scoops vanilla ice cream

PASSIONFRUIT SAUCE

60 ml (2 fl oz/¼ cup) passionfruit pulp

2 tablespoons caster (superfine) sugar

1 **Put the sugar,** vanilla bean and 625 ml (21½ fl oz/2½ cups) of water in a large saucepan. Stir over low heat until the sugar has dissolved. Bring to a slow boil, then add the peaches and simmer for 5 minutes, or until the peaches are just tender and softened. Cool them in the syrup, then remove with a slotted spoon. Peel and halve the peaches, removing the stones.

2 **Put the raspberries** in a food processor, process until puréed, then push through a sieve, discarding the pulp.

3 **To make the passionfruit sauce,** combine the passionfruit pulp with the sugar and stir until the sugar has dissolved.

4 **To serve,** divide the raspberry purée among 4 glasses. Arrange a scoop of ice cream and two peach halves on top. Spoon over the passionfruit sauce and serve immediately.

RASPBERRY AND ORANGE TRIFLE

SERVES 6

500 ml (17 fl oz/2 cups) good-quality
  ready-made custard

250 g (9 oz/1 heaped cup)
  mascarpone cheese

120 g (4¼ oz/½ cup) puréed raspberries

40 g (1½ oz/⅓ cup) icing
  (confectioners') sugar

60 g (2¼ oz/1¼ cups) lightly crushed
  ready-made meringues

250 g (9 oz) sliced plain orange cake or
  4 sliced orange muffins

Sprinkle 60 ml (2 fl oz/¼ cup) orange
  liqueur, such as Cointreau

375 g (13½ oz/3 cups) raspberries

40 g (1½ oz/1¼ cups) crushed
  meringues

icing (confectioners') sugar, to serve,
  if desired

1 Combine the custard, mascarpone cheese, puréed raspberries, icing sugar and meringues.

2 Arrange plain orange cake or sliced orange muffins in the base of a large glass dish or six dessert glasses.

3 Sprinkle orange liqueur over the cake. Top with 250 g (9 oz/2 cups) raspberries. Spoon the custard mixture over the raspberries and top with remaining raspberries and the crushed meringues. Chill until ready to serve. Dust with sifted icing sugar just before serving.

AROMATIC PEACHES WITH SWEETENED GREEK YOGHURT

SERVES 4

225 g (8 oz/1 cup) caster (superfine) sugar

1 vanilla bean, split lengthways

1 cinnamon stick

6 cardamom pods

2 star anise

4 peaches

2 tablespoons dark brown sugar

300 g (10½ oz/1¼ cups) Greek-style yoghurt

1 Pour **500 ml** (17 fl oz/2 cups) of water into a saucepan and add the caster sugar. Heat over medium heat until the sugar has dissolved.

2 **Scrape the seeds** from the vanilla bean into the saucepan and add the pod, cinnamon stick, cardamom pods and star anise. Boil for 2 minutes, then set aside to cool.

3 **Put the peaches** in a heatproof bowl. Cover with boiling water and set aside for 1 minute. Drain the peaches and refresh in ice-cold water. Halve the peaches, removing the stones and skin. Working quickly to prevent the flesh from browning, place the peaches in a bowl and strain the cooled syrup over them. Refrigerate for several hours.

4 **Stir the dark brown sugar** through the yoghurt and serve with the peaches and syrup.

COCONUT PAVLOVAS WITH TROPICAL FRUITS

MAKES 4

PAVLOVAS

2 egg whites, at room temperature

115 g (4 oz/½ cup) caster (superfine) sugar

½ teaspoon cornflour (cornstarch)

½ teaspoon natural vanilla extract

15 g (½ oz/¼ cup) shredded coconut

PASSIONFRUIT CREAM

250 ml (9 fl oz/1 cup) thick (double/ heavy) cream, whipped

2 tablespoons icing (confectioners') sugar

pulp of 4 passionfruit

½ small red papaya, seeded and peeled

4 fresh lychees, halved and seeded

½ mango, peeled and seeded

1　To make the pavlovas, preheat the oven to 120°C (235°F/ Gas ½). Line a baking tray with baking paper.

2　Beat egg whites and sugar in a bowl for 8 minutes, or until the meringue is glossy and very thick. Beat in the cornflour and vanilla extract. Gently fold the shredded coconut through the meringue mixture with a metal spoon.

3　Using two large metal tablespoons, spoon four large oval-shaped spoonfuls of meringue mixture onto the prepared tray. Bake for 30 minutes, or until the pavlovas are crisp on the outside. Turn off the oven and leave the pavlovas in the oven until the oven is cold.

4　To make the passionfruit cream, beat the cream and icing sugar until firm peaks form. Fold the passionfruit pulp through the cream and refrigerate until ready to serve.

5　Cut the papaya, lychees and mango into very small dice.

6　To serve, top the pavlovas with some of the passionfruit cream and accompany with the diced fruit.

Note: For a quick alternative, make the meringues and top with whipped cream, a selection of fresh berries and a quick coulis made from puréed and sieved berries.

RUBY RED GRAPEFRUIT GRANITA

SERVES 4

110 g (3¾ oz/½ cup) sugar

350 ml (12 fl oz) freshly squeezed ruby grapefruit juice

150 ml (5 fl oz) orange muscat dessert wine

1 **Put the sugar** and 125 ml (4 fl oz/½ cup) of water in a small saucepan and bring to the boil. Reduce the heat and simmer for 3–4 minutes, then remove from the heat and set aside to cool.

2 **Combine the grapefruit juice,** wine and cooled sugar syrup in a shallow freezer-proof tray and freeze for 2 hours, or until the mixture has started to freeze around the edges. Break up the mixture with a fork, then return it to the freezer and repeat the process every 30 minutes until the granita has frozen and has a rough, icy texture.

CUSTARDS
& MOUSSES

VANILLA CUSTARDS WITH BERRIES

MAKES 6

375 ml (13 fl oz/1½ cups) milk

250 ml (9 fl oz/1 cup) thick (double/ heavy) cream

1 vanilla bean, split, seeds scraped

175 g (6 oz/¾ cup) caster (superfine) sugar

3 eggs, plus 4 egg yolks

150 g (5½ oz/1¼ cups) raspberries

150 g (5½ oz/1 cup) blueberries

250 g (9 oz/1⅔ cups) small strawberries, halved if too large

2 tablespoons caster (superfine) sugar, extra

1 Preheat the oven to 160°C (315°F/Gas 2–3) and grease six 185 ml (6 fl oz/¾ cup) ramekins. Line a roasting tin with a tea towel (dish towel), then place the ramekins in the tin.

2 Combine the milk, cream and vanilla bean and seeds in a saucepan over medium heat and bring to the boil. Remove from the heat and set aside. Put the sugar, eggs and yolks in a bowl and whisk until smooth, then slowly whisk in the hot milk mixture. Strain through a fine sieve into a measuring cup then pour the custard evenly into the ramekins.

3 Pour enough hot water into the roasting tin to come halfway up the sides of the ramekins. Bake for 45 minutes, or until just firm. Remove ramekins from the tin and cool to room temperature. Cover with plastic wrap and refrigerate overnight.

4 Combine the raspberries, blueberries and strawberries in a saucepan and sprinkle with the extra sugar. Place over medium heat and toss for 3 minutes, or until the sugar has dissolved and the berries are shiny. Remove from the heat.

5 To serve, place the ramekins in a pan of hot water for 1 minute to make them easier to unmould. Invert each one onto a plate, then spoon the berries over the custards and serve immediately.

PEACH YOGHURT MOUSSE

SERVES 4

125 g (4½ oz/1 cup) dried peaches

250 ml (9 fl oz/1 cup) peach nectar

2 teaspoons powdered gelatine

200 g (7 oz/¾ cup) plain yoghurt

2–3 teaspoons honey, to taste

3 egg whites

2 tablespoons toasted flaked almonds, to serve

1 **Put the peaches** and peach nectar in a small saucepan. Cook over low heat, stirring often, for 10 minutes, or until the peaches are soft and pulpy. Set aside to cool for 10 minutes.

2 **Put 2 tablespoons** of hot water in a small bowl and sprinkle the gelatine over the top. Whisk with a fork for 1 minute, or until the gelatine has dissolved.

3 **Put the peach mixture,** gelatine mixture and yoghurt in a blender or small processor fitted with the metal blade. Whizz for 20–30 seconds, or until smooth. Add the honey, to taste, and whizz to combine.

4 **Whisk the egg whites** until firm peaks form. Pour the peach mixture into the egg whites and gently fold through using a metal spoon.

5 **Spoon the mousse** into 4 x 250 ml (9 fl oz/1 cup) parfait glasses and smooth the surface. Cover and refrigerate for at least 1 hour, or until firm. Serve sprinkled with the almonds.

LITTLE CHERRY CUSTARDS

MAKES 6

250 ml (9 fl oz/1 cup) milk

125 ml (4 fl oz/½ cup) thick (double/
heavy) cream

1 vanilla bean, split, seeds scraped

1 cinnamon stick, broken in half

3 eggs

2 egg yolks

140 g (5 oz/⅔ cup) caster
(superfine) sugar

425 g (15 oz) tin pitted cherries, drained,
liquid reserved

115 g (4 oz/½ cup) caster (superfine)
sugar, extra

3 tablespoons kirsch

1 Preheat the oven to 160°C (315°F/Gas 2–3) and lightly grease six 125 ml (4 fl oz/½ cup) dariole moulds.

2 Combine the milk and cream in a saucepan. Add the vanilla bean and seeds and the cinnamon stick and heat until almost at boiling point. Remove from the heat.

3 Put the eggs, egg yolks and sugar in a bowl and whisk to combine. Gradually whisk the hot milk and cream into the egg mixture, then strain into a clean bowl.

4 Place two or three cherries in the base of each mould and fill with the custard mixture. Sit the custards in a roasting tin and pour in enough hot water to come halfway up the sides of the moulds. Cover with foil, pressing around the edges to form a seal, and steam in the oven for 45–50 minutes, or until a skewer comes out clean when inserted in the middle. Remove from the roasting tin and leave the custards to settle for 3 minutes before inverting onto serving plates.

5 Meanwhile, put the reserved cherry liquid, extra sugar and kirsch in a heavy-based frying pan over low heat and stir until the sugar has dissolved. Add the remaining cherries, increase the heat and bring to the boil, then reduce the heat and simmer for 15 minutes, or until the liquid becomes syrupy. Spoon the cherry compote over the custards before serving.

GINGER NUT AND LIME CHEESECAKE POTS

MAKES 6

6 ginger nut biscuits (ginger snaps)

300 ml (10½ fl oz) thick (double/heavy) cream

250 g (9 oz/1 cup) cream cheese, softened

2 eggs

80 g (2¾ oz/⅓ cup) caster (superfine) sugar

2 teaspoons grated lime zest

4 tablespoons lime juice

1 **Preheat the oven** to 160°C (315°F/Gas 2–3). Place a biscuit in the base of six 170 ml (5½ fl oz/⅔ cup) ramekins.

2 **Combine the cream,** cream cheese, eggs, sugar, lime zest and juice in a food processor and blend until smooth. Pour the mixture over the biscuits.

3 **Put the ramekins** in an ovenproof dish and pour in enough water to come a third of the way up the sides of the ramekins. Bake for 50 minutes, or until just firm in the centre and beginning to brown. Remove the cheesecakes from the ovenproof dish and cool to room temperature before serving.

WHITE CHOCOLATE AND CINNAMON MOUSSE

SERVES 4

2 eggs, separated

4 tablespoons milk

1 teaspoon ground cinnamon

180 g (6½ oz/1⅓ cups) white chocolate, chopped

2 teaspoons gelatine powder

185 ml (6 fl oz/¾ cup) thick (double/heavy) cream

150 g (5½ oz/1 cup) fresh blueberries, plus extra to serve

1 **Put the egg yolks,** milk and cinnamon in a small heavy-based saucepan and whisk together. Add the chopped chocolate and stir over low heat until the mixture is smooth.

2 **Put 2 tablespoons** of hot water in a small bowl, and sprinkle the gelatine over the surface. Stand for a few minutes to soften, then whisk with a fork to dissolve. Stir into the warm chocolate mixture. Set over a bowl of cold water to cool.

3 **Using electric beaters,** beat the egg whites until soft peaks form. In a separate bowl, beat the cream until soft peaks form. Fold the cream into the chocolate mixture, then fold in the egg whites.

4 **Divide the blueberries** between serving glasses or bowls. Spoon the chocolate mixture into the serving dishes. Cover and refrigerate for several hours, or until set. Top with extra blueberries and serve.

LEMON AND LIME CURDS

MAKES 6

4 eggs

2 egg yolks

175 g (6 oz/¾ cup) caster (superfine) sugar

100 ml (3½ fl oz) lemon juice

2½ tablespoons lime juice

finely grated zest of 2 limes

300 ml (10½ fl oz) thick (double/heavy) cream

boiling water, for steaming

CANDIED LEMONS

115 g (4 oz/½ cup) caster (superfine) sugar

1 lemon, finely sliced

baby meringues, to serve

thick (double/heavy) cream, to serve

1 **Preheat oven** to 160°C (315°F/Gas 2–3). Line a roasting tin with a tea towel (dish towel). Place six 185 ml (6 fl oz/¾ cup) ramekins in the tin.

2 **Combine the eggs,** egg yolks and sugar in a large bowl and whisk until the sugar has dissolved and the mixture is well combined. Stir in the lemon and lime juice and the lime zest. Add the cream and mix well to combine.

3 **Pour the mixture** into the ramekins, then pour enough boiling water into the roasting tin to come halfway up the side of the ramekins. Bake for 30 minutes, or until just set (the curds should be slightly wobbly when you shake them).

4 **Remove the ramekins** from the roasting tin and allow to cool, then refrigerate until cold.

5 **To make the candied lemons,** put the sugar and 125 ml (4 fl oz/½ cup) of water in a saucepan over medium–high heat and stir until the sugar has dissolved. Add the lemon slices and bring to the boil. Reduce the heat to medium and simmer without stirring for 5–10 minutes, or until the syrup has reduced a little. Remove from the heat and allow to cool. Chill in the refrigerator until ready to serve.

6 **Place a candied lemon slice** on top of each curd. Drizzle with a little syrup. Serve with the baby meringues and cream.

BLUEBERRY CUSTARD CRUMBLES

SERVES 6

300 g (10½ oz/2 cups) blueberries

1 vanilla bean

250 ml (9 fl oz/1 cup) ready-made thick vanilla custard

4 tablespoons thick (double/heavy) cream

2 tablespoons icing (confectioners') sugar, plus extra, for dusting

2 teaspoons finely grated orange zest

150 g (5½ oz) butternut biscuits (cookies)

1 Divide the blueberries among six 185 ml (6 fl oz/¾ cup) ramekins.

2 Split the vanilla bean in half lengthways, then scrape out the seeds and put them in a bowl (reserve the vanilla pod for another use). Add the custard, cream, icing sugar and orange zest and mix together well. Spoon the mixture over the berries.

3 Put the biscuits in a sealed bag and crush them with a rolling pin. Sprinkle the crumbs evenly over the custards and refrigerate for 1 hour.

4 Heat the grill (broiler) to medium. Dredge the tops of the crumbles generously with icing sugar and grill for about 3 minutes, or until lightly browned. Serve hot.

WHITE CHOCOLATE MOUSSE

SERVES 6

150 g (5½ oz/1 cup) roughly chopped white chocolate

50 g (1¾ oz) unsalted butter

1 teaspoon natural vanilla extract

3 eggs, separated

1 egg white

2 tablespoons caster (superfine) sugar

125 ml (4 fl oz/½ cup) thick (double/heavy) cream, whipped

white chocolate shavings, to serve

1 **Put the chocolate** in a small processor fitted with the metal blade and whizz for 15 seconds, or until finely chopped.

2 **Melt the butter** and vanilla extract in a small saucepan over low heat. Add to the processor containing the chocolate and whizz for 8–10 seconds, or until the chocolate has melted and the mixture is smooth. With the motor running, add the egg yolks one at a time and whizz until just combined. Transfer to a large bowl.

3 **Put the four egg** whites in a large processor fitted with the whisk attachment and whisk until soft peaks form. With the motor running, gradually add the caster sugar and whisk until stiff peaks form. (This step can also be done using electric beaters.) Fold a spoonful of the egg whites into the chocolate mixture, then gently fold in the remaining egg whites.

4 **Very carefully fold the whipped cream** through the chocolate mixture until it is well combined.

5 **Divide the mixture** among six bowls, cover with plastic wrap and refrigerate overnight.

6 **Serve each mousse** topped with a sprinkling of white chocolate shavings.

BAKED CUSTARD TARTS WITH RHUBARB

MAKES 8

2 quantities sweet shortcrust pastry
(see page 156)

½ vanilla bean or ½ teaspoon natural
vanilla extract

250 ml (9 fl oz/1 cup) milk

250 ml (9 fl oz/1 cup) pouring cream

4 eggs

145 g (5½ oz/⅔ cup) caster (superfine)
sugar

400 g (14 oz/3 cups) rhubarb, trimmed,
then cut into 2 cm (¾ inch) pieces

80 g (2¾ oz/⅓ cup) soft brown sugar

½ teaspoon ground cinnamon

1 teaspoon lemon juice

1 **Preheat the oven** to 200°C (400°F/Gas 6). Lightly grease eight loose-based tartlet tins, 10 cm (4 inches) in diameter and 3 cm (1¼ inches) deep.

2 **Roll out the pastry** on a lightly floured work surface to 3 mm (⅛ inch) thick. Cut the pastry into rounds to fit the base and sides of the tins. Gently press in the sides to fit, trim the edges, then cover with plastic wrap and refrigerate for 30 minutes.

3 **Line each of the pastry shells** with a crumpled piece of baking paper and fill with baking beads or uncooked rice. Bake the pastry for 15 minutes, then remove the paper and beads and bake for 7–8 minutes, or until the pastry is golden. Reduce the oven to 160°C (315°F/Gas 2–3).

4 **If using the vanilla bean,** split it down the middle and scrape out the seeds.

5 **Combine the milk,** cream, vanilla bean and seeds (or vanilla extract) in a saucepan, then bring just to the boil.

6 **Whisk the eggs** and sugar in a bowl until thick and pale. Pour the milk mixture onto the egg mixture, whisking to combine well. Cool the custard, then strain into a bowl. Pour the custard into the tartlet shells and bake for 25–30 minutes, or until the filling has just set. Remove from the oven.

7 **Increase the oven** to 180°C (350°F/Gas 4). Put the rhubarb, brown sugar, cinnamon, lemon juice and 2 teaspoons water in a small baking dish, toss to combine, then cover with foil and bake for 30 minutes.

8 **Remove the tartlets** from the tins and just before serving spoon on the rhubarb and juices. Serve warm or at room temperature.

CUSTARD SAUCES

MAKES ABOUT 500 ML (17 FL OZ/2 CUPS)

CREME ANGLAISE

4 egg yolks
115 g (4 oz/½ cup) caster (superfine) sugar
200 ml (7 fl oz) milk
200 ml (7 fl oz) pouring cream
1 vanilla bean cut in half (or 1 teaspoon natural vanilla extract).

ORANGE CUSTARD

4 egg yolks
115 g (4 oz/½ cup) caster (superfine) sugar
200 ml (7 fl oz) milk
200 ml (7 fl oz) pouring cream
1 vanilla bean cut in half (or 1 teaspoon natural vanilla extract).
1 tablespoon finely grated orange zest
80 ml (2½ fl oz/⅓ cup) orange-flavoured liqueur

ESPRESSO CUSTARD

4 egg yolks
115 g (4 oz/½ cup) caster (superfine) sugar
200 ml (7 fl oz) milk
200 ml (7 fl oz) pouring cream
1 vanilla bean cut in half (or 1 teaspoon natural vanilla extract).
25 g (1 oz/⅓ cup) whole coffee beans
2½ tablespoons coffee-flavoured liqueur

Crème anglaise: Whisk egg yolks and caster sugar in a bowl until thick and pale. Combine milk and pouring cream in a saucepan. Split vanilla bean in half, scrape out the seeds and add the bean and seeds to the saucepan (alternatively, if you don't have a vanilla bean, substitute 1 teaspoon natural vanilla extract). Slowly bring almost to the boil. Strain the milk mixture onto the egg yolk mixture, stirring to combine. Discard the vanilla bean. Return the mixture to a clean saucepan, then cook over medium–low heat, stirring constantly with a wooden spoon until the mixture is thick enough to coat the back of the spoon. Do not allow the mixture to boil or the custard will curdle. Serve the custard hot, warm or chilled. If serving chilled, lay plastic wrap directly on the surface of the custard to prevent a skin forming. Refrigerate for up to 2 days. Serve with fresh fruit tarts, especially ones that contain pears, apples or cherries..

Orange custard: Make one quantity of crème anglaise. Add finely grated orange zest to the milk mixture. Strain the milk mixture onto the egg yolk mixture, and continue to cook the custard, as above. Stir orange-flavoured liqueur into the cooled custard. The flavour of this custard goes well with desserts such as rhubarb slice or prune clafoutis.

Espresso custard: Make one quantity of crème anglaise, as above. Add whole coffee beans to the milk mixture, then strain through a sieve after the custard has thickened. Stir coffee-flavoured liqueur into the cooled custard, if desired. This is delicious served with coffee-flavoured baked puddings or flourless chocolate cake.

BAKED CHOCOLATE CUSTARDS

SERVES 10

30 g (1 oz) unsalted butter, melted

55 g (2 oz/¼ cup) caster (superfine) sugar, for dusting

300 ml (10½ fl oz) pouring cream

200 ml (7 fl oz) milk

200 g (7 oz/1½ cups) dark chocolate, roughly chopped

grated zest from 1 orange

6 eggs

115 g (4 oz/½ cup) caster (superfine) sugar, extra

icing (confectioners') sugar, for dusting

raspberries, to serve

1 **Preheat the oven** to 160°C (315°F/Gas 2–3). Grease ten 125 ml (4 fl oz/½ cup) ramekins or ovenproof moulds with butter and dust the inside of each with sugar.

2 **Put the cream and milk** in a saucepan over low heat and bring almost to the boil.

3 **Add the chocolate** and stir over low heat until the chocolate has melted and is well combined. Stir in the orange zest.

4 **Whisk the eggs and sugar** in a large bowl for 5 minutes, or until pale and thick. Whisk a little of the hot chocolate cream into the eggs, then pour the egg mixture onto the remaining chocolate cream, whisking continuously.

5 **Divide the mixture** among the ramekins. Put the custards in a large roasting tin and pour in enough hot water to come halfway up the sides of the ramekins. Cover the tin with foil and bake for 30–35 minutes, or until the custards are set. Immediately remove the ramekins from the water bath. Set aside to cool completely.

6 **Turn out onto a serving dish**, top with the raspberries and dust with icing sugar.

CREAM CHEESE SOUFFLÉS

MAKES 6

50 g (1¾ oz) unsalted butter, melted

55 g (2 oz/¼ cup) caster (superfine) sugar, for dusting

250 g (9 oz/1 cup) cream cheese

55 g (2 oz/¼ cup) caster (superfine) sugar, extra

3 eggs, separated

2 tablespoons plain (all-purpose) flour

500 ml (17 fl oz/2 cups) milk

1 tablespoon Grand Marnier or other orange liqueur

finely grated zest from 1 orange

icing (confectioners') sugar, for dusting

3 oranges, peeled and segmented, to serve

---

1 Preheat the oven to 200°C (400°F/Gas 6). Grease six 250 ml (9 fl oz/1 cup) soufflé dishes with the melted butter and dust with the sugar.

2 Combine the cream cheese, extra sugar and egg yolks in a heatproof bowl and beat using electric beaters until very smooth. Stir in the flour.

3 Combine the milk, Grand Marnier and orange zest in a saucepan and bring almost to boiling point.

4 Whisk the milk mixture into the cream cheese mixture, stir until smooth, then return to a clean saucepan. Stir constantly over very low heat for 5–7 minutes, or until the custard thickens slightly; do not allow the custard to boil.

5 Whisk the egg whites in a clean, dry bowl until stiff peaks form, then gently fold into the warm custard mixture.

6 Place the prepared soufflé dishes on an oven tray. Fill the dishes two-thirds full with the soufflé mixture. Cook for 15 minutes, or until the soufflés are well risen and firm to the touch.

7 Serve immediately dusted with icing sugar and with the orange segments.

MALAY GOW

**MAKES 4 INDIVIDUAL CAKES
OR 1 LARGE CAKE**

2 eggs

95 g (3¼ oz/½ cup firmly packed) soft
brown sugar

4 tablespoons evaporated milk

60 g (2¼ oz) butter, melted

90 g (3¼ oz/¾ cup) self-raising flour

½ teaspoon bicarbonate of soda
(baking soda)

maple syrup, to serve (optional)

whipped cream, to serve (optional)

1 Lightly grease and line the bases of four 250 ml
(9 fl oz/1 cup) ramekins or one 20 cm (8 inch) cake tin.

2 Put the eggs and sugar in a small bowl and beat with
electric beaters for about 5 minutes, or until thick. Stir in the
evaporated milk and melted butter. Fold in the flour and
bicarbonate of soda. Divide the mixture evenly among the
ramekins or pour into the cake tin.

3 Arrange the ramekins in a bamboo steamer. Sit the
steamer over a wok of boiling water and steam, covered, for
20–25 minutes, or until cooked through. If making one large
cake, cover the tin with foil and put on a steaming rack in
the wok. Steam for 35–40 minutes, or until cooked.

4 These cakes are best served warm, so if you have made
them ahead of time, steam them again just before eating.
They are delicious served drizzled with maple syrup and a
dollop of cream on the side.

LIME CREME BRULEE WITH RASPBERRIES

SERVES 4

500 ml (17 fl oz/2 cups) thick (double/heavy) cream

1 teaspoon finely grated lime zest

½ teaspoon vanilla extract

5 egg yolks

4 tablespoons caster (superfine) sugar

2 tablespoons demerara or soft brown sugar

150 g (5½ oz/1¼ cups) raspberries

1 **Put the cream** and lime zest in a saucepan and bring to the boil over low heat. Stir in the vanilla.

2 **Meanwhile,** using electric beaters, beat the egg yolks and caster sugar in a bowl until the sugar has dissolved and the mixture is light, thick and starts to hold its shape.

3 **Beating slowly,** gradually pour the hot cream into the egg mixture. Put in a double boiler or in a heatproof bowl over a pan of simmering water and stir for about 10 minutes, or until the mixture coats the back of a wooden spoon. Pour into four 125 ml (4 fl oz/½ cup) ramekins, then cover and refrigerate the custards overnight.

4 **Heat the grill** (broiler) to high. Sprinkle the demerara sugar evenly over the custards. Sit the ramekins in a shallow ovenproof dish, pack ice around them, then place the dish on the grill tray. Grill for 2 minutes, or until the sugar has melted, checking to see that it doesn't burn. Leave the ramekins in the ice for 1–2 minutes to allow the sugar to harden and the custards to set. Sit the raspberries on top and serve.

CARDAMOM AND YOGHURT BAVAROIS

MAKES 8

4 egg yolks

115 g (4 oz/½ cup) caster (superfine) sugar

200 g (7 oz) vanilla yoghurt

185 ml (6 fl oz/¾ cup) milk

1 teaspoon ground cardamom

½ teaspoon natural vanilla extract

1 tablespoon gelatine powder

300 ml (10½ fl oz) cream, lightly whipped

1 Beat the egg yolks and sugar until the mixture is thick and pale.

2 Combine the yoghurt, milk, cardamom and vanilla in a saucepan and stir over low heat until just coming to the simmer. Pour the warm milk mixture over the yolks and whisk to combine. Return to a clean saucepan and stir over medium heat for 8 minutes, or until the custard has thickened enough to coat the back of a wooden spoon. Remove from the heat.

3 Dissolve the gelatine in 3 tablespoons of hot water and stir it through the custard.

4 Set the custard aside to cool completely, then gently fold through the cream.

5 Divide the mixture between 8 x 125 ml (4 fl oz/½ cup) ramekins and refrigerate for 2–3 hours to set.

6 To unmould and serve, dip a blunt knife into warm water and run the tip around the edge of the mould. Dip the mould into a bowl of warm water for a few seconds, shaking slightly to loosen. Place the serving plate over the mould, invert and remove the mould.

STEAMED COCONUT CARAMEL CUSTARDS

SERVES 4

175 g (6 oz/¾ cup) caster (superfine) sugar

CUSTARD

4 eggs, lightly beaten

55 g (2 oz/¼ cup) caster (superfine) sugar

400 ml (14 fl oz) tin coconut cream

30 g (1 oz/⅓ cup) desiccated coconut, lightly toasted

fresh fruit and cream, to serve

1 **Combine the sugar** and 250 ml (9 fl oz/1 cup) of water in a small saucepan. Stir over low heat until the sugar dissolves, then bring to the boil. Cook without stirring for 10–12 minutes, or until the mixture turns lightly golden. Remove from the heat and pour the caramel into four 250 ml (9 fl oz/1 cup) ramekins. Working quickly, gently tilt to coat the base and sides. Take care as the ramekins will get hot.

2 **To make the custard,** combine the egg, sugar, coconut cream and desiccated coconut. Strain through a fine sieve, then divide the custard among the caramel-coated ramekins. Cover each with foil.

3 **Put the ramekins** in a bamboo steamer. Sit the steamer over a wok of simmering water and steam, covered, for 20–25 minutes, or until the custard is set. Alternatively, put a wire rack in a wok and pour in boiling water to just below the rack. Sit the ramekins on top, cover with a lid or sheet of foil and steam for 20–25 minutes.

4 **Allow to cool,** then put the custards in the refrigerator for at least 2 hours or overnight. Before serving, run a blunt knife around the edge and flip out onto a serving plate. Serve with fresh fruit and cream.

Note: Allow about 125 ml (4 fl oz/½ cup) of custard per serve.

STRAWBERRY AND MASCARPONE MOUSSE

SERVES 6

80 g (2¾ oz/⅓ cup) caster (superfine) sugar

1 tablespoon powdered gelatine

500 g (1 lb 2 oz/3⅓ cups) strawberries, hulled

250 g (9 oz/1 cup) mascarpone cheese

crushed praline to serve (optional)

1 **Combine the sugar** and 125 ml (4 fl oz/½ cup) of water in a small saucepan. Stir over low heat for 3 minutes, or until the sugar has dissolved. Sprinkle the gelatine over the sugar mixture and stir for 2 minutes, or until the gelatine has dissolved. Set aside to cool.

2 **Put the hulled strawberries** in a food processor and process until smooth. Add the mascarpone and process until well combined. With the motor running, add the gelatine mixture in a slow stream. Pour the mixture into a 1 litre (35 fl oz/4 cup) mould. Refrigerate overnight, or until set.

3 **To serve,** dip the base of the mould in hot water for 10 seconds, then invert the mousse onto a plate. Top with the crushed praline, if using.

NUTMEG AND SAFFRON PANNA COTTA

MAKES 6

500 ml (17 fl oz/2 cups) thick (double/heavy) cream
185 ml (6 fl oz/¾ cup) milk
100 g (3½ oz/scant ½ cup) caster (superfine) sugar
1 teaspoon ground nutmeg
pinch saffron threads
2½ teaspoons gelatine powder
fresh seasonal fruit, to serve

1 Put the cream, milk, sugar, nutmeg and saffron in a saucepan. Heat over low heat until the mixture just comes to the boil. Remove from the heat immediately and cool until just warm.

2 Place 2 tablespoons of hot water in a small bowl, and sprinkle the gelatine over the surface. Stand for a few minutes to soften, then whisk with a fork to dissolve. Stir into the cream mixture and leave to cool.

3 When cool, strain the mixture and pour into 6 x 125 ml (4 fl oz/½ cup) dariole moulds. Refrigerate overnight to set.

4 To unmould and serve, dip a blunt knife into warm water and run the tip around the edge of the mould. Dip the mould into a bowl of warm water for a few seconds, shaking slightly to loosen. Place the serving plate over the mould, invert and remove the mould. Repeat with the other moulds. Serve the panna cotta with fresh fruit.

VANILLA BUTTERMILK PANNA COTTA WITH SUMMER FRUITS

SERVES 4

PANNA COTTA

2 teaspoons powdered gelatine

250 ml (9 fl oz/1 cup) cream (whipping)

55 g (2 oz/¼ cup) caster (superfine) sugar

½ vanilla bean, split lengthways

250 ml (9 fl oz/1 cup) buttermilk

pulp of 2 passionfruit

2 teaspoons caster (superfine) sugar

½ small pineapple, peeled and cored

½ small red papaya, seeded and peeled

1 **To make** the panna cotta, lightly grease 4 x 125 ml (4 fl oz/½ cup) metal, glass or ceramic moulds.

2 **Put** 2 teaspoons of water in a small bowl and sprinkle with the gelatine. Leave the gelatine to sponge and swell.

3 **Put the cream,** sugar and vanilla bean in a small saucepan and stir over low heat for 2–3 minutes, or until the sugar has dissolved. Whisk the gelatine mixture into the cream mixture until the gelatine has dissolved. Set aside to infuse for 3 minutes.

4 **Scrape the seeds** from the vanilla bean into the cream mixture, discarding the vanilla pod.

5 **Pour the mixture** into a bowl. Shake the buttermilk carton well before measuring, then whisk the buttermilk into the cream mixture.

6 **Divide the mixture** among the prepared moulds. Put the moulds on a tray, cover with plastic wrap and refrigerate for 3–4 hours, or until set.

7 **Sieve the passionfruit pulp** into a small bowl, discarding the seeds. Stir in the sugar.

8 **Cut the pineapple** and papaya into long thin slivers.

9 **To serve,** gently run a small blunt knife around the side of each mould and turn the panna cotta out onto large serving plates. If they don't readily come out, briefly dip the moulds in a bowl of hot water. Arrange the fruit slivers around the panna cotta and drizzle with the passionfruit juice.

HONEY CHOCOLATE MOUSSE

SERVES 6

225 g (8 oz) Toblerone®

50 g (2 oz) block milk chocolate, at room temperature

60 ml (2 fl oz/¼ cup) warm water

180 ml (6 fl oz/¾ cup) cream

3 egg whites

blueberries, to garnish

1 Place the chocolate and warm water in a medium heatproof bowl over a pan of simmering water. Stir until melted. Remove from heat.

2 Using electric beaters, beat cream in medium bowl until soft peaks form.

3 Beat the egg whites in a small bowl until stiff peaks form. Using a metal spoon, fold egg whites into cream.

4 Gently fold half the cream mixture into the chocolate mixture until both are combined, then fold in remaining cream mixture.

5 Spoon into 6 individual dessert dishes or ramekins. Refrigerate for 6 hours.

6 To serve, top the mousse with fresh berries. Make chocolate shavings by running a vegetable peeler firmly down the sides of a chocolate block. Sprinkle over the berries to decorate.

Note: Mousse may be made up to 8 hours in advance. Refrigerate until required.

FROZEN

STRAWBERRY AND STAR ANISE SORBET

SERVES 4

115 g (4 oz/½ cup) caster
(superfine) sugar

3 star anise

750 g (1 lb 10 oz/5 cups) strawberries

3 tablespoons lime juice

1 Put 250 ml (9 fl oz/1 cup) of water and the sugar and star anise in a small saucepan over low heat and stir until the sugar has dissolved. Increase the heat and boil for 1 minute. Set aside to cool completely. Discard the star anise.

2 Hull and purée the strawberries. Combine the purée, lime juice and cold sugar syrup in a bowl and stir to combine.

3 Pour the mixture into an ice cream maker and churn according to the manufacturer's instructions until the sorbet is just firm. Spoon into a container and freeze until ready to serve.

MANGO AND LIME GELATO

SERVES 4–6

235 g (8½ oz/1 cup) caster (superfine) sugar

2 large ripe mangoes, chopped (see Note)

60 ml (2 fl oz/¼ cup) lime juice

1 teaspoon grated lime zest

1 **Put the sugar** and 500 ml (17 fl oz/2 cups) of water in a small saucepan and stir over medium–low heat until the sugar has dissolved. Bring to the boil, then reduce heat and simmer for 10 minutes. Remove from the heat and cool almost to room temperature.

2 **Put the mango** in a blender or small processor fitted with the metal blade and whizz for 20 seconds, or until puréed. Add the cooled sugar syrup and lime juice. Whizz for 30 seconds, or until thoroughly blended. Pour into a shallow metal tin and stir in the lime zest.

3 **Freeze the mixture** for 1½ hours, or until almost frozen.

4 **Whizz again** in the blender or processor to break up the ice crystals, then return to the freezer in the tin until completely frozen.

5 **Use a metal spoon** to scoop the gelato into glasses or bowls and serve.

Note: You will need 750 g (1 lb 10 oz/3½ cups) of mango flesh for this recipe.

RASPBERRY SEMIFREDDO

SERVES 6–8

235 g (8½ oz/2 cups) raspberries
(see Note), plus extra for serving

110 g (3¾ oz/1 cup) icing
(confectioners') sugar

1½ tablespoons lime juice

200 g (7 oz/¾ cup) Greek-style yoghurt

300 ml (10½ fl oz/1 ⅓ cup) thick
(double/heavy) cream

wafers, to serve

1 Put the raspberries, sugar, lime juice and yoghurt in a blender and whizz for 20–25 seconds, or until smooth.

2 Whisk the cream in a bowl until soft peaks form. Gently fold the raspberry mixture into the cream. Pour into a shallow metal tin, cover with plastic wrap or foil and freeze for 1–1½ hours, or until the edges are frozen.

3 Line a 1 litre (35 fl oz/4 cup) loaf (bar) tin with plastic wrap so that it overhangs the edges. Return the raspberry mixture to the blender and whizz for 6–10 seconds, or until smooth. Transfer to the prepared tin and smooth the top. Fold the plastic wrap over the top and freeze for at least 4 hours, or until set.

4 Remove the tin from the freezer and leave at room temperature for 2–3 minutes. Lift the semifreddo from the tin using the plastic wrap and cut into slices. Sandwich between 2 wafers that have been trimmed to fit. Serve with extra raspberries.

Note: Either fresh raspberries or thawed frozen raspberries will provide a good result.

CARDAMOM COFFEE ICE CREAM

SERVES 4

6 green cardamom pods

375 ml (13 fl oz/1½ cups) milk

250 ml (9 fl oz/1 cup) thick (double/ heavy) cream

1 tablespoon instant coffee granules

115 g (4 oz/½ cup) caster (superfine) sugar

5 egg yolks

1 **Lightly crush the cardamom pods** and put in a saucepan with the milk, cream and coffee granules. Heat gently until the mixture just reaches boiling point. Remove from the heat and leave to infuse for 20 minutes.

2 **In a bowl,** beat the sugar and egg yolks together until pale and light, stir in the infused cream mixture and strain into a clean saucepan. Heat gently, stirring constantly over low heat for 10 minutes, or until the mixture thickens to coat the back of the spoon. Do not allow the custard to boil or it will curdle.

3 **Remove from the heat** and leave to cool completely. Pour into a shallow container, cover and freeze until frozen around the edges. Put into a cold bowl and beat with electric beaters until thick. Return to the shallow container and refreeze. Repeat this process 2–3 times until the ice cream is a thick consistency. Pour into a container and freeze.

4 **If using an ice-cream machine,** chill the mixture for 1 hour and then churn in an ice cream maker until frozen.

5 **Serve** at once or freeze in a plastic container until required.

BLOOD ORANGE AND CHAMPAGNE SORBET

SERVES 6–8

115 g (4 oz/½ cup) caster
(superfine) sugar

500 ml (17 fl oz/2 cups) blood orange
juice (see Note)

150 ml (5 fl oz) Champagne

2 tablespoons Campari

1 Put the sugar and 250 ml (9 fl oz/1 cup) of water in a heavy-based saucepan. Stir constantly over medium–low heat until the sugar has dissolved, then stop stirring. Bring to the boil, then reduce the heat and simmer for 5 minutes. Cool.

2 Put the sugar syrup, blood orange juice, Champagne and Campari in a blender or processor fitted with the plastic blade. Whizz for 15–20 seconds, or until thoroughly combined. Pour into ice cube trays and freeze for 2 hours, or until firm.

3 Turn the frozen mixture out of the trays and return to the blender or processor. Whizz in 5-second bursts until the mixture forms a coarse, icy purée. Transfer to a plastic container and return to the freezer for 1 hour.

4 Remove the sorbet from the freezer and break it up with a fork. Work quickly, as it will melt quickly.

5 Spoon the sorbet into bowls or glasses and serve immediately.

Note: You will need about six oranges to make 500 ml (17 fl oz/2 cups) of juice. If blood oranges are not in season, use other oranges.

CINNAMON SEMIFREDDO

SERVES 8–10

230 g (8½ oz/1 cup) caster (superfine) sugar

4 eggs, at room temperature, separated

600 ml (21 fl oz/2⅓ cups) thick (double/ heavy) cream

1½ teaspoons ground cinnamon

pinch salt

tinned baby apples, or fresh seedless grapes or cherries, to serve (optional)

1 **Line** a 21 x 11 x 7 cm (8¼ x 4¼ x 2¾ inch) loaf (bar) tin with a double layer of plastic wrap, allowing the excess to overhang onto the sides.

2 **Using electric beaters,** beat the sugar and egg yolks in a bowl until thick and pale.

3 **In a separate bowl,** whisk the cream to soft peaks, then gently fold through the egg yolk mixture along with the cinnamon.

4 **In a separate bowl,** whisk the egg whites with the salt until firm peaks form. Gently fold through the mixture. Pour into the prepared tin and cover with a double layer of plastic wrap. Place in the freezer overnight, or until firm.

5 **Transfer the semifreddo** from the freezer to the refrigerator 5 minutes before serving. Turn out onto a board, remove the plastic wrap and cut into slices. Serve with baby apples, if desired.

VANILLA-SCENTED RHUBARB ICE

SERVES 8

650 g (1 lb 7 oz) rhubarb (about 6 stems)

230 g (8½ oz/1 cup) caster (superfine) sugar

1 vanilla bean

whipped cream, to serve (optional)

1 Wash the rhubarb and trim the ends. Chop the stems into 2 cm (¾ inch) lengths, and put into a saucepan. Add the sugar and 250 ml (9 fl oz/1 cup) water, and stir over a low heat until the sugar has dissolved.

2 Split the vanilla bean in half lengthways, and scrape out the seeds. Add the seeds and bean to the pan.

3 Bring to the boil and cook over a medium–low heat, partially covered, for 5 minutes, until the rhubarb is very soft. Cool slightly, remove the vanilla bean, then purée in a food processor until smooth.

4 Pour into a 1.25 litre (44 fl oz/5 cup) capacity plastic container, cover tightly and freeze for 4 hours. Use a fork to break up the crystals, and freeze again for another 4 hours.

5 To serve, break up the crystals again with a fork, then spoon into small serving glasses. Drizzle a little cream over, and serve immediately.

COFFEE GRANITA WITH CRUSHED COFFEE BEANS

SERVES 8–10

300 g (10½ oz/1⅓ cups) sugar

1 litre (35 fl oz/4 cups) freshly made
espresso coffee

55 g (2 oz/⅓ cup) chocolate-coated
coffee beans

1 **Stir the sugar** into the hot coffee until the sugar has dissolved. Allow to cool. Transfer to a deep plastic container.

2 **Freeze the mixture** for 1–2 hours, or until ice crystals have formed around the edges. Using an immersion blender or blender, whizz for 15–20 seconds to break up the ice crystals. Return to the freezer and repeat this method every 30 minutes or so until the mixture reaches a coarse snowy texture.

3 **Put the chocolate-coated coffee beans** in a mini processor or coffee grinder and whizz briefly until roughly ground.

4 **Serve the granita** in chilled glasses topped with a sprinkling of the beans.

MANGO ICE CREAM LOG

SERVES 8–10

500 ml (17 fl oz/2 cups) thick (double/heavy) cream

250 ml (9 fl oz/1 cup) milk

1 vanilla bean, split lengthways

6 egg yolks, at room temperature

115 g (4 oz/½ cup) caster (superfine) sugar

2 large mangoes, flesh puréed

1 **Put the cream and milk** in a saucepan. Scrape the seeds from the vanilla bean into the saucepan and add the vanilla pod. Heat over medium heat until the mixture is hot but not boiling. Remove from the heat and discard the vanilla pod.

2 **Using electric beaters,** beat the egg yolks and caster sugar in a large bowl until thick and pale. Slowly pour the hot cream mixture onto the egg mixture, whisking continuously. Pour the custard into a clean saucepan and stir over low heat for 5–6 minutes, or until the custard is thick enough to coat the back of a spoon. Refrigerate until completely cold.

3 **Pour the custard** into an ice-cream machine and churn according to the manufacturer's instructions. Alternatively, pour the custard into a metal bowl and freeze for 2–2½ hours, or until set around the edges but still soft in the middle; beat with electric beaters for 3 minutes, or until the custard is smooth again. Once the mixture is churned or smooth, pour half the mixture into an 8 x 19 cm (3¼ x 7½ inch) loaf (bar) tin lined with plastic wrap. Refrigerate the remaining mixture until required. Carefully spoon the mango purée over the mixture in the tin and freeze for 1 hour. Top with the remaining ice cream mixture and freeze overnight.

4 **To serve,** dip the base of the tin in hot water for 5 seconds, then invert ice cream onto a serving plate and cut into slices.

LYCHEE AND STRAWBERRY ICE CREAM

SERVES 6–8

250 g (9 oz/1⅔ cups) strawberries

165 g (5¾ oz/¾ cup) caster (superfine) sugar

565 g (1 lb 4 oz) tin lychees in syrup

375 ml (13 fl oz/1½ cups) milk

500 ml (17 fl oz/2 cups) thick (double/heavy) cream

6 egg yolks, at room temperature

1 Reserve 50 g (1¾ oz/½ cup) of the strawberries for decoration. Hull and roughly chop the remaining strawberries and place in a bowl, along with any juices. Sprinkle with 1 tablespoon of the sugar and set aside for 30 minutes. Drain and finely chop the lychees, reserving 125 ml (4 fl oz/½ cup) of the syrup.

2 Put the milk, cream and remaining sugar in a saucepan over medium heat. Cook, stirring constantly, for a few minutes, or until the sugar has dissolved and the milk is just about to boil. Remove from the heat.

3 Whisk the egg yolks in a bowl for 1 minute, or until combined, then add 60 ml (2 fl oz/¼ cup) of the hot milk mixture. Stir to combine, then pour into the remaining milk mixture. Return the saucepan to low–medium heat and cook, stirring constantly with a wooden spoon, until the mixture thickens and coats the back of the spoon. Do not allow the mixture to boil. Strain through a fine sieve and set aside to cool.

4 Gently stir the strawberries and any juice, lychees and lychee syrup into the custard to combine. Transfer to an ice-cream machine and freeze according to the manufacturer's instructions. Alternatively, transfer to a shallow metal tray and freeze, whisking every couple of hours until the ice cream is frozen and creamy in texture. Serve the ice cream with the reserved strawberries.

PEACH AND ROSEWATER SORBET

SERVES 4–6

400 ml (14 fl oz) peach tea

300 g (10½ oz/1⅓ cups) caster (superfine) sugar

6 peaches

80 ml (2½ fl oz/⅓ cup) rosewater

1 **Pour half the peach tea** into a small saucepan. Add the sugar and stir until the sugar has dissolved. Bring to the boil and cook for 2 minutes, then remove from the heat and set aside to cool.

2 **Quarter the peaches,** removing the stones. Put the peaches and remaining peach tea in a saucepan and poach for 10 minutes. Remove the peaches with a slotted spoon, reserving the liquid, and peel off the skin. Set aside to cool.

3 **Using a hand blender** or small food processor, purée the peaches, poaching liquid, sugar syrup and rosewater until smooth. Pour the mixture into a plastic container and freeze for 1½ hours, or until the sides and base have frozen and the middle is a soft slush.

4 **Using a food processor** or hand blender, process until the mixture is evenly slushy. Repeat the freezing and processing at least twice, then freeze for another 30–60 minutes.

TURKISH DELIGHT ICE CREAM

SERVES 6

375 ml (13 fl oz/1½ cups) milk

500 ml (17 fl oz/2 cups) thick (double/heavy) cream

150 g (5½ oz/⅔ cup) caster (superfine) sugar

6 egg yolks, at room temperature

100 g (3½ oz) Turkish delight, roughly chopped

2 tablespoons pomegranate seeds

1 Put 250 ml (9 fl oz/1 cup) of the milk in a saucepan with the cream and sugar. Cook over medium heat, stirring constantly for a few minutes, until the sugar has dissolved and the milk is just about to boil. Remove from the heat.

2 Whisk the egg yolks in a bowl for 1 minute, or until combined, then add 60 ml (2 fl oz/¼ cup) of the hot milk mixture. Stir to combine, then pour into the remaining milk mixture. Return the saucepan to low–medium heat and cook, stirring constantly with a wooden spoon, until the mixture thickens and coats the back of the spoon. Do not allow the mixture to boil. Strain through a fine sieve and set aside to cool.

3 Put the remaining milk and the Turkish delight in a small saucepan over medium heat. Stir constantly until the Turkish delight has dissolved into the milk. Stir into the custard mixture and set aside to cool.

4 Transfer the mixture to an ice-cream machine to churn and freeze according to the manufacturer's instructions. Alternatively, transfer to a shallow tray and freeze, whisking every couple of hours until frozen to give the ice cream a creamy texture.

5 Serve the ice cream topped with the pomegranate seeds.

PLUM AND BISCOTTI ICE CREAM

SERVES 4

450 g (1 lb) plums

80 g (2¾ oz/⅓ cup) caster (superfine) sugar

almond extract, a few drops

500 ml (17 fl oz/2 cups) good-quality ready-made custard

80 g (2¾ oz) almond biscotti, chopped

1   Halve the plums, removing the stones. Combine the sugar and 125 ml (4 fl oz/½ cup) of water in a saucepan. Add the plums and poach for 10 minutes. Set aside to cool.

2   Purée the plums, poaching liquid and almond extract until smooth. Carefully stir the plum mixture into the custard. Pour the mixture into a shallow plastic container and freeze for 1–1½ hours, or until the sides and base have frozen and the centre is a soft slush.

3   Using a hand blender or electric whisk, blend or beat the plum mixture until it is uniformly slushy. Return the mixture to the freezer, repeating the blending process at least twice.

4   Stir in the biscotti and freeze for another 30–60 minutes, or until the ice cream is firm.

RUBY PLUM SORBET

SERVES 6

150 ml (5 fl oz) freshly squeezed
    orange juice

grated zest of 1 orange

185 g (6½ oz/¾ cup) caster
    (superfine) sugar

820 g (1 lb 13 oz) tin whole plums,
    drained

¼ teaspoon ground cinnamon

1 **Put the orange juice,** orange zest, sugar and 150 ml (5 fl oz) of water in a saucepan. Stir over medium heat until the sugar has dissolved. Bring to the boil, then remove from the heat and set aside to cool.

2 **Halve the plums** and discard the seeds. Strain the orange syrup into a blender. Add the plums and cinnamon and whizz for 2–3 minutes, or until very smooth.

3 **Pour the mixture** into a 28 x 19 cm (11¼ x 7½ inch) shallow metal tin, cover with plastic wrap or foil and freeze for 1–1½ hours, or until the mixture starts to freeze around the edges. Return to the blender and whizz for 6–10 seconds, or until the mixture is smooth. Return to the tin, cover and freeze for 1 hour. Blend once more, then freeze until ready to serve.

CAKES

CHOCOLATE STAR ANISE CAKE WITH COFFEE CARAMEL

SERVES 8

200 g (7 oz/1⅓ cups) good-quality dark
chocolate, roughly chopped

125 g (4½ oz) unsalted butter

4 eggs

2 egg yolks

115 g (4 oz/½ cup) caster
(superfine) sugar

50 g (1¾ oz) plain (all-purpose)
flour, sifted

2 teaspoons ground star anise

50 g (1¾ oz/½ cup) ground almonds

COFFEE CARAMEL CREAM

125 ml (4 fl oz/½ cup) thick (double/
heavy) cream

3 tablespoons soft brown sugar

2 tablespoons brewed espresso coffee,
cooled

1 **Preheat the oven** to 190°C (375°F/Gas 5). Grease and line a 23 cm (9 inch) springform cake tin.

2 **Put the chocolate** and butter in a bowl set over a saucepan of gently simmering water, but do not allow the base of the bowl to come into contact with the water. Heat gently until the mixture is melted.

3 **Put the eggs,** egg yolks and sugar into a bowl and beat with electric beaters for 5 minutes until thickened. Fold in the flour, ground star anise and ground almonds and then fold in the melted chocolate mixture until evenly combined (the mixture should be runny at this stage).

4 **Pour the mixture** into the prepared tin and bake for 30–35 minutes, or until a skewer inserted in the middle comes out clean. Cool in the tin for 5 minutes and then remove and cool on a wire rack.

5 **To make the coffee caramel cream,** whip the cream, sugar and coffee together until soft peaks form and the colour is a soft caramel.

6 **Serve** the cold cake cut into wedges with a spoonful of the coffee caramel cream.

APRICOT MERINGUE TORTE

SERVES 8–10

375 g (13 oz/1⅔ cups) caster (superfine) sugar
1 cinnamon stick
2 teaspoons natural vanilla extract
450 g (1 lb) apricots, quartered, stones removed
6 egg whites, at room temperature
1½ teaspoons white vinegar
35 g (1¼ oz/⅓ cup) ground hazelnuts
300 ml (10½ fl oz) thick (double/heavy) cream
icing (confectioners') sugar, for dusting

1   Combine 375 ml (13 fl oz/1½ cups) of water, 125 g (4½ oz/heaped ½ cup) of the sugar, the cinnamon stick and 1 teaspoon of the vanilla in a large saucepan. Stir over low heat until the sugar has dissolved. Increase the heat to medium and simmer for 15 minutes. Add the quartered apricots and simmer over low heat for another 40 minutes, or until the apricots are thick and pulpy. Set aside to cool.

2   **Preheat the oven** to 150°C (300°F/Gas 2) and draw a 22 cm (8½ inch) circle on two sheets of baking paper. Put the sheets, pencil side down, on two baking trays.

3   **Beat the egg whites** in a bowl until stiff peaks form. Add the remaining sugar, a little at a time, and continue beating until the mixture is stiff and glossy. Beat in the vinegar and remaining vanilla. Gently fold in the ground hazelnuts.

4   **Divide the meringue** mixture between the two circles on the prepared trays and smooth the surface. Bake for 35–40 minutes, or until the meringues are firm and dry. Turn off the oven and leave the meringues in the oven to cool completely.

5   **Peel off the baking paper** and place one meringue disc on a serving plate. Whip the cream until stiff peaks form. Discard the cinnamon stick from the syrup and drain the apricots. Gently stir the apricots through the whipped cream and spread over the meringue. Place the second meringue disc on top of the apricot cream and dust with icing sugar.

BAUMKUCHEN

SERVES 6

100 g (3½ oz) marzipan

100 g (3½ oz) butter, softened

80 g (2¾ oz/⅓ cup) caster (superfine) sugar, plus 2 tablespoons extra

1 teaspoon finely grated lemon zest

1 teaspoon natural vanilla extract

4 eggs, separated

60 g (2¼ oz/½ cup) plain (all-purpose) flour

60 g (2¼ oz/½ cup) cornflour (cornstarch)

2 tablespoons apricot jam, sieved and warmed

icing (confectioners') sugar, for dusting

GLAZE

100 ml (3½ fl oz) thick (double/heavy) cream

140 g (5 oz/1 cup) dark chocolate, chopped

fresh mixed berries, to serve

thick (double/heavy) cream (optional), to serve

1 Heat the grill (broiler) to high. Chop 30 g (1 oz) of the marzipan and put it in a small bowl with the butter and sugar. Beat with hand-held electric beaters until light and fluffy, then beat in the lemon zest, vanilla and egg yolks. Sift in the flour and cornflour and stir until combined.

2 In a separate small bowl, beat the egg whites with electric beaters until soft peaks form. Gradually add the extra 2 tablespoons of sugar, beating until dissolved. Fold the egg whites into the marzipan mixture in two batches.

3 Mark a 20 cm (8 inch) square on a sheet of baking paper. Spread 125 ml (4 fl oz/ ½ cup) of the cake mixture into the square. Put the sheet under the grill and cook for 2 minutes, or until the cake layer is well browned. Remove from the grill, allow to cool slightly, then spread the cake layer with another 125 ml (4 fl oz/½ cup) of the cake mixture. Return to the grill and cook again until well browned. Allow to cool slightly, then

repeat the layering and grilling process until all of the mixture is used up. When you're finished, allow the cake to cool.

4 Trim the edges of the cake to form a neat square, then cut the cake in half to form two rectangles. Generously spread one of the rectangles with some of the jam, then sandwich the other half over the top. Spread remaining jam over the top and sides.

5 Dust a work surface with icing sugar and roll out the remaining marzipan until it is wafer thin. Use it to cover the top and sides, then sit the cake on a cake rack set in a tray.

6 To make the glaze, heat the cream in a small saucepan until almost boiling. Put the chocolate in a bowl, pour on the hot cream and stir gently until the chocolate has melted. Pour the mixture evenly over the cake, using a spatula to spread it. Leave for 30 minutes to set (you can place it in the refrigerator, if necessary). Decorate with mixed berries and serve.

ALMOND FUDGE CHEESECAKE WITH GINGER CRUST

SERVES 6–8

CRUST

185 g (6½ oz) ginger nut biscuits (ginger snaps), roughly broken

60 g (2¼ oz) butter, melted

FILLING

750 g (1 lb 10 oz/3 cups) cream cheese, softened

250 g (9 oz/1 cup) raw or golden caster (superfine) sugar

3 eggs

½ teaspoon natural almond extract

2 teaspoons natural vanilla extract

TOPPING

185 g (6½ oz/1 cup) dark chocolate chips

60 g (2¼ oz) butter

60 g (2¼ oz/⅔ cup) toasted flaked almonds

1 Preheat the oven to 180°C (350°F/Gas 4). Grease a 22 cm (8½ inch) spring-form cake tin and line base with baking paper.

2 To make the crust, put the biscuits in a large processor fitted with the metal blade. Whizz for 20–25 seconds, or until the biscuits form fine crumbs. Add the melted butter and whizz for 8–10 seconds, or until combined. Press the crust firmly over the base of the prepared tin. Chill until firm.

3 To make the filling, wipe out the processor bowl and add the cream cheese. Whizz for 20–25 seconds, or until smooth, scraping down the side of the bowl as needed. Add the sugar, eggs, almond extract and vanilla and whizz in 5-second bursts for 15–20 seconds, or until well blended.

4 Pour the filling into the prepared tin. Bake for 45 minutes, or until set. Turn off the oven, prop the door slightly ajar and leave to cool for 30 minutes, then remove from the oven and cool completely.

5 To make the topping, put the chocolate and butter in a small heatproof bowl. Place over a saucepan of simmering water, ensuring that the water doesn't touch the bottom of the bowl. Heat, stirring occasionally, until melted and smooth. Stir in the almonds.

6 Spread the topping over the top of the cheesecake and allow to set before serving.

CHESTNUT, GINGER AND PISTACHIO LOAF

SERVES 10–12

200 g (7 oz/1⅓ cups) roughly chopped
 dark chocolate

110 g (3¾ oz) butter, chopped

875 g (1 lb 15 oz) chestnut purée

40 g (1½ oz/⅓ cup) icing
 (confectioners') sugar

60 ml (2 fl oz/¼ cup) mandarin liqueur
 or orange liqueur

60 g (2¼ oz/⅓ cup) roughly chopped
 preserved ginger

70 g (2½ oz/½ cup) pistachio nuts

70 g (2½ oz/½ cup) toasted slivered
 almonds

extra icing (confectioners') sugar,
 to serve

1 Put the chocolate and butter in a heatproof bowl and place over a saucepan of simmering water, ensuring that the water doesn't touch the bottom of the bowl. Heat, stirring occasionally, for 5–6 minutes, or until melted and smooth. Remove from the heat and set aside to cool for 10 minutes.

2 Put the chestnut purée, sugar and 2 tablespoons of the liqueur in a large processor fitted with the metal blade and whizz until smooth. Add the chocolate mixture and whizz until smooth. Add the ginger and half the pistachios and almonds. Whizz in 5-second bursts until the nuts are roughly chopped.

3 Line the base and two opposite sides of an 8 x 16 cm (3¼ x 6¼ inch) loaf (bar) tin with foil, allowing the foil to overhang the sides to help remove the loaf from the tin. Mix the remaining liqueur with 1 tablespoon of water and brush over the inside of the tin. Spoon the chestnut mixture into the tin, packing it down tightly to eliminate air pockets. Fold the foil overhang over the surface and cover with plastic wrap. Refrigerate for at least 3 hours, or until firm.

4 Using the foil handles, lift the loaf out of the tin. Peel off and discard the foil. Put the loaf on a serving plate, scatter the remaining nuts over the top and dust with icing sugar.

5 Cut into slices to serve.

FIG SHORTCAKE

SERVES 12

185 g (6½ oz/1½ cups) plain (all-purpose) flour

60 g (2¼ oz/½ cup) self-raising flour

2 teaspoons ground cinnamon

1 teaspoon ground ginger

1 teaspoon mixed (pumpkin pie) spice

115 g (4 oz/½ cup) soft brown sugar

55 g (2 oz/½ cup) ground hazelnuts

125 g (4½ oz) unsalted butter, chopped

1 egg, lightly beaten

315 g (11¼ oz/1 cup) fig jam

95 g (3½ oz/⅔ cup) hazelnuts, toasted and finely chopped

icing (confectioners') sugar, for dusting (optional)

whipped cream, to serve (optional)

1 **Preheat the oven** to 180°C (350°F/Gas 4). Grease a 35 x 11 cm (14 x 4¼ inch) loose-based rectangular shallow tart tin.

2 **Combine the flours**, spices, sugar and ground hazelnuts in a food processor and process to just combine. Add the butter and, using the pulse button, process in short bursts until crumbly. Add the egg, a little at a time, until the mixture comes together; you may not need all the egg. Divide the dough in half, wrap separately in plastic wrap and refrigerate for 30 minutes.

3 **Remove one ball of dough** from the refrigerator and roll out between two sheets of baking paper, large enough to fit the base and sides of the tin. Line the tin, gently pressing to fit into the corners, and patching any holes with extra dough, if necessary. Trim away the excess.

4 **Spread the pastry** with the fig jam. Using the second chilled ball of dough, coarsely grate it into a bowl, add the chopped hazelnuts and gently toss to combine. Press the mixture gently over the top of the jam, taking care to retain the grated texture. Bake for 35 minutes, or until golden brown. Cool completely in the tin before cutting, and dust lightly with icing sugar to serve.

5 **Serve** with whipped cream, if desired.

Note: Fig shortcake will keep, stored in an airtight container, for up to 4 days, or up to 3 months in the freezer.

PASSIONFRUIT CREAM SPONGE ROLL

SERVES 8

4 eggs, separated

175 g (6 oz/¾ cup) caster (superfine) sugar

1 teaspoon natural vanilla extract

90 g (3¼ oz/¾ cup) cornflour (cornstarch)

3 tablespoons plain (all-purpose) flour

1½ teaspoons baking powder

boiling water, for steaming

2 tablespoons icing (confectioners') sugar, for dusting

PASSIONFRUIT CREAM

310 ml (10¾ fl oz/1¼ cups) whipped cream

3 tablespoons icing (confectioners') sugar, sifted

2 tablespoons passionfruit pulp (about 2 passionfruit)

1 Preheat the oven to 180°C (350°F/Gas 4) and line a 29 x 24 x 3 cm (11½ x 9½ x 1¼ inch) Swiss roll tin (jelly roll tin) with baking paper.

2 Using electric beaters, beat the egg whites and a pinch of salt until soft peaks form. Gradually beat in the sugar until the mixture is thick and glossy. Add the egg yolks and vanilla extract, and beat until well combined.

3 In a separate bowl, mix together the cornflour, plain flour and baking powder. Sift the flours twice, then carefully fold into the egg mixture. Don't over-stir as the cake will lose its light texture.

4 Pour the mixture into the prepared tin and smooth with a spatula. Cover with foil, then place the tin in a large deep roasting tin and pour in enough boiling water to come halfway up the sides of the Swiss roll tin. Bake for 35–45 minutes, or until golden and springy to the touch. Cool in the tin for 1 minute, then run a knife around the edges of the tin to loosen the sponge cake. Place a large piece of baking paper on a clean surface. Invert the cake onto the baking paper then gently peel away the baking paper from the bottom of the cake. Using the baking paper as a guide, gently roll the cake into a log, starting from the long side. This needs to be done while the cake is still hot to prevent cracking. Leave to cool for 20 minutes.

5 Meanwhile, to make the passionfruit cream, whip the cream and icing sugar until stiff, then fold in the passionfruit pulp. Gently unroll the cake and spread with the passionfruit cream. Re-roll, then dust with icing sugar and serve at once.

Note: This is best eaten on the day it is made.

ORANGE AND ALMOND POPPY SEED CAKES

MAKES 4

1 orange

100 g (3½ oz/1 cup) ground almonds

80 g (2¾ oz/⅓ cup) caster (superfine) sugar

1 tablespoon poppy seeds

1 teaspoon baking powder

2 eggs, lightly beaten

ORANGE SAUCE

thin strips of zest from 1 orange

4 tablespoons fresh orange juice

55 g (2 oz/¼ cup) caster (superfine) sugar

2 tablespoons chunky orange marmalade

cream or ice cream, to serve

1 Put the orange in a saucepan with enough water to cover. Bring to the boil, then reduce the heat and simmer for about 45 minutes, ensuring the orange stays covered with water. Drain, refresh under cold water, then leave to cool. Cut into quarters and remove the pips. Put the skin and flesh in a food processor and process until smooth.

2 Preheat the oven to 180°C (350°F/Gas 4). Grease and line the bases of four giant muffin holes with baking paper. Put an ovenproof dish in the oven and half-fill with hot water.

3 In a large bowl combine ground almonds, sugar, poppy seeds and baking powder, then stir in the egg and orange purée. Pour into the prepared muffin holes and smooth the surfaces. Cover with a sheet of well-greased baking paper.

4 Put the muffin tin in the ovenproof dish and bake for 30 minutes, or until the cakes are firm to the touch and come away from the sides a little. Remove from the oven and leave for 5 minutes before turning out of the tin. Peel off the paper.

5 Meanwhile, to make the orange sauce, put the orange zest, juice and sugar in a saucepan over low heat and stir until the sugar has dissolved. Stir in the marmalade, increase the heat and boil for 5 minutes, or until thick and syrupy.

6 Serve the cakes face down, topped with the orange sauce and a little cream or ice cream. These are delicious warm or at room temperature.

CRUSTLESS REDCURRANT CHEESECAKE

SERVES 6–8

150 g (5½ oz/1¼ cups) toasted slivered almonds

750 g (1 lb 10 oz) neufchatel cheese

2 tablespoons plain (all-purpose) flour

300 g (10½ oz/1⅓ cups) caster (superfine) sugar

2 teaspoons natural vanilla extract

1½ teaspoons finely grated lemon zest

4 eggs

125 g (4½ oz/1 cup) redcurrants, plus extra to serve

2 teaspoons crème de cassis or cherry brandy

1 tablespoon icing (confectioners') sugar

TOPPING

300 g (10½ oz/1¼ cups) sour cream

2 tablespoons caster (superfine) sugar

1 teaspoon natural vanilla extract

1 **Preheat the oven** to 170°C (325°F/Gas 3). Grease a 22 cm (8½ inch) spring-form cake tin. Put the almonds in a large processor fitted with the metal blade and whizz in 2-second bursts for 12 seconds, or until they resemble fine breadcrumbs. Do not grind the almonds to a powder. Transfer the almonds to the prepared tin and roll the tin around to coat with the almonds. Spread the excess almonds over the base of the tin.

2 **Put the neufchatel cheese,** flour, caster sugar, vanilla and lemon zest in the cleaned processor. Whizz for 12–15 seconds, or until smooth. Add the eggs and whizz for 10 seconds, or until well combined, scraping down the side of the bowl as needed. Transfer the mixture to a bowl.

3 **Without cleaning the processor bowl,** add redcurrants, crème de cassis or cherry brandy and icing sugar and whizz for about 10–12 seconds, or until the mixture is smooth.

4 **Add 250 ml** (9 fl oz/1 cup) of the cheese mixture and briefly whizz to combine.

5 **Gently pour** the remaining cheese mixture into the tin, being careful not to disturb the almond crumbs. Bake for 20 minutes. Gently spoon the redcurrant mixture over the surface and bake for a further 30 minutes, or until the surface is just set. Remove from the oven and set aside to cool for 15 minutes.

6 **To make the topping,** mix the sour cream, sugar and vanilla in a small bowl until smooth. Spread the mixture over the cheesecake and return to the oven for 10 minutes. Leave to cool in the tin, then turn out and chill until serving.

7 **Serve** topped with extra redcurrants.

PEAR AND PECAN DESSERT CAKE

SERVES 6–8

50 g (1¾ oz/½ cup) pecans

300 g (10½ oz) dried pears

150 g (5½ oz) unsalted butter

175 g (6 oz/¾ cup) caster (superfine) sugar

1 teaspoon natural vanilla extract

3 eggs

185 g (6½ oz/1½ cups) plain (all-purpose) flour

2 teaspoons baking powder

½ teaspoon ground cinnamon

½ teaspoon ground ginger

2 tablespoons milk

BROWN SUGAR SYRUP

150 g (5½ oz/⅔ cup) soft brown sugar

1 teaspoon ground cinnamon

4 tablespoons brandy

60 g (2¼ oz) unsalted butter, softened

whipped cream, to serve

---

1 Preheat the oven to 180°C (350°F/Gas 4). Grease and line a 24 cm (9½ inch) round cake tin, then arrange the pecans in the base of the tin.

2 Cover the dried pears with warm water and leave for about 10–15 minutes, or until softened. Pat dry with paper towels.

3 Using electric beaters, beat the butter and sugar until light and fluffy. Add the vanilla and the eggs one at a time, beating well after each addition. Sift the flour, baking powder, cinnamon and ginger into a bowl, add to the cake mixture and beat slowly to combine. Add the milk and beat for a further minute.

4 To make the brown sugar syrup, combine the sugar, cinnamon, brandy and butter in a small saucepan over medium heat and cook for 3 minutes, or until the sugar has dissolved.

5 Pour the warm syrup over the nuts in the cake tin. Arrange the pears over the nuts. Spoon the cake mixture over the pears and smooth the surface with a spatula. Cover the cake tin with a large square of foil, then place the cake tin a large roasting tin. Pour in enough hot water to come halfway up the side of the cake tin, then bake for 40 minutes. Remove the foil and bake for a further 15 minutes, or until golden and cooked through when tested with a skewer.

6 Leave the cake in the tin for 5 minutes, then carefully invert onto a plate and serve warm with whipped cream.

LIME CAKES WITH BLACKBERRIES

SERVES 4

185 g (6½ oz/1½ cups) self-raising flour

½ teaspoon baking powder

55 g (2 oz/¼ cup) caster (superfine) sugar

grated zest of 1 lime

2 eggs

185 ml (6 fl oz/¾ cup) buttermilk

20 g (¾ oz) butter, melted

BLACKBERRY SAUCE

300 g (10½ oz/scant 1⅓ cups) caster (superfine) sugar

1 tablespoon lime juice

1 tablespoon raspberry liqueur (optional)

150 g (5½ oz/1 cup) blackberries

thick (double/heavy) cream, to serve

1   Grease four 250 ml (9 fl oz/1 cup) rum baba tins or ramekins. Sift the flour and baking powder into a large bowl and mix in the sugar and lime zest. Make a well in the centre, add the eggs and buttermilk and whisk until combined. Stir in the melted butter.

2   Spoon the mixture into the prepared tins. Place a piece of greased baking paper over the top of each, then wrap tightly in foil.

3   Place the tins in a steamer and cover with a lid. Sit the steamer over a saucepan or wok of boiling water and steam for 20 minutes, or until risen and firm to the touch.

4   To make the blackberry sauce, combine the sugar and 200 ml (7 fl oz) of water in a saucepan over low heat and stir until the sugar has dissolved. Bring to the boil, then reduce the heat and simmer without stirring for 15–20 minutes, or until slightly thickened. Add the lime juice, liqueur and blackberries and simmer gently for 5 minutes, or until the syrup takes on the colour of the blackberries. Cool slightly.

5   Turn the puddings out onto individual plates and spoon the fruit and syrup over the top. Serve hot with cream.

ORANGE AND PRUNE RICE CAKE

SERVES 8

1 vanilla bean or 1 teaspoon natural
vanilla extract

200 g (7 oz/1 cup) medium-grain rice

1 litre (35 fl oz/4 cups) milk

1 fresh bay leaf, bruised

2½ teaspoons finely grated orange zest

4 eggs, lightly beaten

170 g (6 oz/¾ cup) caster
(superfine) sugar

200 g (7 oz) fresh ricotta cheese

60 g (2¼ oz/½ cup) slivered almonds

PRUNE FILLING

200 g (7 oz) pitted prunes

115 g (4 oz/½ cup) caster
(superfine) sugar

125 ml (4 fl oz/½ cup) sweet Marsala

whipped cream, to serve

1 To make the prune filling, put the prunes in a heatproof bowl with 625 ml (21½ fl oz/ 2½ cups) boiling water. Leave for 30 minutes. Put the prune mixture in a saucepan with the sugar and Marsala and slowly bring to the boil. Reduce heat to low and simmer for 15 minutes, or until the prunes are very soft. Cool the prunes in the liquid. Strain, reserving the liquid.

2 Split vanilla bean down the middle and scrape out the seeds. Put the bean and seeds in a pan with the rice, milk and bay leaf. Gently bring to a simmer. Cook, covered, over low heat for 20 minutes, or until rice is tender and the liquid mostly absorbed. Cover. Cool slightly. Discard bay and vanilla bean.

3 Preheat the oven to 170°C (325°F/Gas 3). Lightly grease an 18 cm (7 inch) round spring-form cake tin and line the base with baking paper. Wrap a piece of foil tightly around the base and up the outside of the tin to completely seal it.

4 Combine the orange zest, eggs, sugar, ricotta (and vanilla extract, if using) in a bowl and, using a wooden spoon, stir until smooth. Add the egg mixture to the rice and stir to combine well. Pour half of the rice mixture into the prepared tin and smooth the top. Arrange the prunes on top, pour over the remaining mixture and scatter over the almonds.

5 Put the cake tin in a roasting tin and pour in enough boiling water to come halfway up the side of the cake tin. Bake for 50 minutes, or until the cake is firm in the centre. Cover the cake with foil halfway through cooking if it browns too quickly.

6 Meanwhile, put the reserved prune liquid into a small saucepan and bring to the boil. Reduce the heat to low and simmer for 15 minutes, or until the liquid has reduced by one-third. Cool the rice cake in the tin. Turn out onto a serving plate and serve with whipped cream and the syrup.

PISTACHIO AND LIME SEMOLINA CAKE WITH DATE GLAZE

SERVES 16

DATE GLAZE

185 g (6½ oz/heaped ¾ cup) caster (superfine) sugar

200 g (7 oz/1¼ cups) pitted dates, roughly chopped

2 limes, juiced

125 g (4½ oz) unsalted butter, softened

125 g (4½ oz/heaped ½ cup) caster (superfine) sugar

2 limes, zest finely grated

2 eggs, at room temperature

360 g (12¾ oz/3 cups) fine semolina

90 g (3¼ oz/⅔ cup) pistachio nuts chopped

2 teaspoons baking powder

½ teaspoon bicarbonate of soda (baking soda)

185 g (6½ oz/¾ cup) plain yoghurt

125 ml (4 fl oz/½ cup) milk

crème fraîche or thick (double/heavy) cream, to serve

1   **To make the date glaze,** put the sugar in a small pan with 185 ml (6 fl oz/¾ cup) of water. Stir over medium heat until the sugar has dissolved. Add the dates and the lime juice and bring to the boil. Reduce the heat and simmer for 6–8 minutes, or until the dates have softened. Remove from the heat and set aside to cool.

2   **Preheat the oven** to 180°C (350°F/Gas 4). Grease and line a 23 cm (9 inch) square cake tin.

3   **Put the butter,** sugar and lime zest in a large bowl and beat with electric beaters until light and fluffy. Add the eggs, one at a time, beating well after each addition.

4   **In a separate bowl,** combine the semolina, pistachios, baking powder and bicarbonate of soda. Stir the semolina mixture and yoghurt alternately through the butter mixture, then stir in the milk. Pour mixture into the prepared tin and bake for 40 minutes, or until a skewer comes out clean when inserted in the centre of the cake.

5   **Spoon the date glaze** over the hot cake in the tin and place on a wire rack to cool.

6   **Serve** the cake warm or at room temperature, accompanied by crème fraîche or thick cream.

SUNKEN CHOCOLATE DESSERT CAKES

SERVES 4

1 tablespoon melted unsalted butter

115 g (4 oz/½ cup) caster (superfine) sugar, plus 1 tablespoon extra

150 g (5½ oz/1 cup) dark chocolate, chopped

125 g (4½ oz) butter

3 eggs

30 g (1 oz/¼ cup) plain (all-purpose) flour

ice cream, to serve

1 **Preheat the oven** to 180°C (350°F/Gas 4). Grease four 250 ml (9 fl oz/1 cup) ramekins with the melted butter and coat lightly with the extra sugar.

2 **Put the chocolate** and butter in a small heatproof bowl. Sit the bowl over a small saucepan of simmering water, stirring frequently until the chocolate and butter have melted. Take care that the base of the bowl doesn't touch the water. Remove from the heat.

3 **Whisk the eggs** and sugar in a bowl using electric beaters until the mixture is pale and thick. Sift the flour onto the egg mixture, then whisk the flour into the mixture. Whisk in the melted chocolate.

4 **Divide the batter** among the prepared ramekins and place on a baking tray. Bake for 30–35 minutes, or until set and firm to touch. Allow cakes to cool in the ramekins for 10 minutes before turning out onto serving plates (if they are reluctant to come out, run a knife around the inside edge of the ramekins to loosen them).

5 **Serve** warm with ice cream. Alternatively, serve in the ramekins, dusted with icing (confectioners') sugar.

WHITE CHOCOLATE AND BERRY ROULADE

SERVES 6–8

4 eggs, at room temperature, separated

115 g (4 oz/½ cup) caster (superfine) sugar, plus extra, for sprinkling

1 tablespoon hot water

60 g (2¼ oz/heaped ⅓ cup) white chocolate finely grated

60 g (2¼ oz/½ cup) self-raising flour

100 g (3½ oz/⅔ cup) strawberries sliced

100 g (3½ oz/heaped ¾ cup) fresh raspberries

1–2 tablespoons caster (superfine) sugar, or to taste

185 ml (6 fl oz/¾ cup) thick (double/ heavy) cream

2 teaspoons icing (confectioners') sugar, plus extra, for dusting

1 teaspoon natural vanilla extract

1 **Preheat the oven** to 200°C (400°F/Gas 6). Lightly spray or grease a 25 x 30 cm (10 x 12 inch) Swiss roll tin (jelly roll tin) with oil. Line the tin with baking paper, allowing the paper to hang over the two long sides.

2 **Beat the egg yolks and sugar** with electric beaters for 5 minutes, or until very thick and creamy. Fold in the hot water and grated white chocolate. Sift the flour over the mixture and gently fold through until just combined.

3 **Beat the egg whites** with clean electric beaters until soft peaks form. Using a large metal spoon, fold the egg whites through the chocolate mixture until just combined. Pour the mixture into the prepared tin and bake for 12–15 minutes, or until the roulade is golden brown and firm to the touch.

4 **Put a large sheet** of baking paper on a flat surface and sprinkle with caster sugar. Turn the roulade out onto the paper. Trim any crisp edges and roll up from the short end with the aid of the baking paper. Leave for 5 minutes, then unroll and allow to cool.

5 **Meanwhile,** put the berries in a bowl and sweeten with the remaining sugar, or to taste. Beat the cream, icing sugar and vanilla until firm peaks form. Spread the roulade with the cream and sprinkle the berries over the top. Roll up and dust with icing sugar. Cut into slices to serve.

CHERRY CHEESECAKE

SERVES 8–10

540 g (1 lb 3 oz) cherries, pitted and halved

125 g (4½ oz/heaped ½ cup) caster (superfine) sugar

2 tablespoons lemon juice

200 g (7 oz) sweet shortbread biscuits (cookies)

90 g (3¼ oz) unsalted butter, melted

500 g (1 lb 2 oz/2 cups) cream cheese, softened

125 g (4½ oz/heaped ⅓ cup) honey

2 natural vanilla extract teaspoons

1 lemon, zest finely grated

4 eggs, at room temperature

200 ml (7 fl oz) thick (double/heavy) cream

1 Put 100 ml (3½ fl oz) of water in a saucepan with the cherries, sugar and lemon juice. Bring to the boil, then reduce heat to low. Cook, stirring occasionally and lightly pressing the cherries to crush them, for 12–15 minutes, or until the cherries are soft and there are 2–3 tablespoons of syrup left. Remove from the heat and set aside to cool.

2 Preheat the oven to 180°C (350°F/Gas 4). Lightly grease a 22 cm (8½ inch) spring-form cake tin. Line the base. Crush the biscuits in a food processor until they form fine crumbs. Add the butter and process until combined. Press mixture into the base of the prepared tin and freeze for 10 minutes. Cover the outside of the tin with strong foil to prevent water seepage during cooking. Place the tin in a deep roasting tin.

3 Beat the cream cheese, honey, vanilla and lemon zest until smooth. Add the eggs, one at a time, beating well after each addition. Stir in the cream. Pour the mixture over the crumb base. Pour enough hot water into the roasting tin to come halfway up the side of the cake tin. Bake 45 minutes, or until almost set. Carefully spoon the cherry mixture over the cheesecake, lightly spreading it to the edge.

4 Bake for 10 minutes, or until just set. Discard the foil, place the cheesecake on a wire rack to cool in the tin, then refrigerate until ready to serve.

5 Allow the cheesecake to return to room temperature before serving.

CARDAMOM, ORANGE AND PLUM DESSERT CAKES

MAKES 8

185 g (6½ oz) unsalted butter, chopped

95 g (3¼ oz/½ cup) soft brown sugar

115 g (4 oz/½ cup) caster (superfine) sugar

3 eggs

1 teaspoon finely grated orange zest

310 g (11 oz/2½ cups) self-raising flour, sifted

1 teaspoon ground cardamom

185 ml (6 fl oz/¾ cup) milk

4 tinned plums, drained and patted dry, cut in half

1 tablespoon raw (demerara) sugar

thick (double/heavy) cream, to serve

1 **Preheat the oven** to 180°C (350°F/Gas 4). Lightly grease eight 250 ml (9 fl oz/1 cup) ceramic ramekins and dust with flour, shaking out any excess flour.

2 **Cream the butter** and sugars in a bowl using electric beaters until pale and fluffy. Add the eggs, one at a time and beating well after each addition, then stir in the orange zest. Fold the flour and cardamom into the butter mixture alternately with the milk until combined and smooth.

3 **Divide the mixture** between the ramekins and place a plum half, cut side down, on top of the batter. Sprinkle with raw sugar, place the ramekins on a baking tray and bake for 30–35 minutes, or until golden and firm to the touch.

4 **Serve** warm or at room temperature with thick cream.

BAKED PASSIONFRUIT CHEESECAKE

SERVES 6–8

60 g (2¼ oz/½ cup) plain (all-purpose) flour

30 g (1 oz/¼ cup) self-raising flour

50 g (1¾ oz) unsalted butter

2 tablespoons caster (superfine) sugar

grated zest from 1 lemon

2 tablespoon lemon juice

FILLING

600 g (1 lb 5 oz) cream cheese, softened

170 g (6 oz/¾ cup) caster (superfine) sugar

30 g (1 oz/¼ cup) plain (all-purpose) flour

125 ml (4 fl oz/½ cup) strained passionfruit juice

4 eggs

170 ml (5½ fl oz/⅔ cup) pouring cream

1 Combine the flours, butter, sugar and lemon zest in a food processor. Add the lemon juice and, using the pulse button, process until a dough forms. Cover with plastic wrap and refrigerate for 1 hour.

2 Meanwhile, preheat the oven to 180°C (350°F/Gas 4). Grease a 22 cm (8½ inch) round spring-form cake tin.

3 Roll out the pastry to 5 mm (¼ inch) thick. Roll the pastry around the pin, lift and ease it into the tin, pressing to fit. Trim the edges. Refrigerate for 10 minutes. Bake for 15–20 minutes, or until golden. Remove from the oven and cool. Reduce the oven to 150°C (300°F/Gas 2).

4 To make the filling, using electric beaters, beat the cream cheese and sugar until smooth. Add the flour and passionfruit juice and beat until combined. Add the eggs one at a time, beating well after each addition. Stir in the cream, then pour the mixture over the cooled base.

5 Bake for 1 hour, or until the centre of the cake is just firm to the touch (move the cheesecake to the lowest shelf of the oven for the last 10 minutes of cooking and cover with foil to prevent overbrowning). Cool the cheesecake in the tin before removing and serving in slices.

Note: You will need about 6 passionfruit to obtain 125 ml (4 fl oz/½ cup) passionfruit juice. Tinned passionfruit pulp is not an adequate substitute.

PASTRY

CARAMELIZED PINEAPPLE AND GINGER TARTE TATIN

SERVES 6–8

165 g (5¾ oz/1⅓ cups) plain (all-purpose) flour

1½ teaspoons ground ginger

85 g (3 oz) unsalted butter, cut into cubes

1 egg yolk

50 g (1¾ oz) glacé ginger, chopped

100 g (3½ oz) unsalted butter, extra

160 g (5¾ oz/scant ¾ cup) caster (superfine) sugar

1 pineapple, peeled, quartered lengthways, cored and cut into 5 mm (¼ inch) slices

thick (double/heavy) cream, to serve

1 Put the flour, ginger and butter in a food processor and process until the mixture resembles fine breadcrumbs. Add the egg yolk, glacé ginger and 2–3 tablespoons of water and pulse until the mixture comes together. Turn out onto a lightly floured surface and bring together in a ball. Cover with plastic wrap and place in the fridge for 20 minutes to rest.

2 Melt the extra butter in a 24 cm (9½ inch) ovenproof frying pan over low heat, add the sugar and stir until dissolved. Increase heat to medium and cook, stirring, until the sugar starts to caramelize and turn golden brown (the mixture may go grainy, but then will go smooth). Reduce the heat to medium–low and add the pineapple slices. Cook for about 15 minutes, or until the pineapple is tender and the caramel mixture is reduced and thickened slightly.

3 Preheat the oven to 180°C (350°F/Gas 4). Roll out the pastry between two sheets of baking paper to a disc slightly larger than the top of the frying pan. Lay the pastry over the top of the pineapple and tuck the edges down the side of the pan. Cook in the preheated oven for 35–40 minutes, or until the pastry is golden in colour.

4 Carefully turn the tart onto a large serving plate, cut into slices and serve with cream.

BERRY AND VANILLA BRULEE TART

SERVES 6–8

SWEET SHORTCRUST PASTRY

250 g (9 oz/2 cups) plain (all-purpose) flour

125 g (4½ oz) unsalted butter, cut into cubes

2 tablespoons caster (superfine) sugar

BERRY CUSTARD FILLING

2 egg yolks

250 ml (9 fl oz/1 cup) thick (double/heavy) cream

125 ml (4 fl oz/½ cup) milk

1 vanilla bean, split lengthways

55 g (2 oz/¼ cup) caster (superfine) sugar

60 g (2¼ oz/½ cup) fresh raspberries

80 g (2¾ oz/½ cup) fresh blueberries

55 g (2 oz/¼ cup) caster (superfine) sugar, for sprinkling

1 **To make the sweet shortcrust pastry,** put the flour and butter in a food processor. Process in short bursts until the mixture resembles fine breadcrumbs. Briefly pulse in the sugar. With the motor still running, add 2 tablespoons of iced water, adding a little more water, if necessary, until the dough comes roughly together. Turn out and press into a ball. Wrap in plastic wrap and refrigerate for at least 30 minutes.

2 **Preheat the oven** to 200°C (400°F/Gas 6). Heat a baking tray. Roll the pastry between two sheets of baking paper. Fit into a 23 cm (9 inch) flan tin with removable base. Line the pastry with a sheet of baking paper and weigh down with rice and/or baking beads. Bake for 15 minutes on the preheated hot tray until lightly golden. Remove the paper and rice and/or baking beads and cook for a further 10 minutes. Reduce the oven temperature to 170°C (325°F/Gas 3). Cool the pastry case.

3 **To make the brûlée filling,** lightly beat together the egg yolks and cream in a bowl. Put the milk, vanilla bean and sugar in a saucepan and stir over low heat until the sugar has dissolved. Increase the heat and bring to the boil. Remove the vanilla bean and scrape the seeds with a knife. Whisk into the hot milk, together with the combined eggs and cream.

4 **Scatter the berries** over the base of the pastry. Carefully pour the custard over the berries. Place on a hot baking tray and bake for 35–40 minutes, or until the custard has set. Cool then refrigerate to firm.

5 **Preheat the grill (broiler).** Sprinkle the pie evenly with the sugar. Place under the hot grill for 7–8 minutes, or until the sugar has melted and caramelized. Cool and cut into wedges to serve.

STRAWBERRY AND RHUBARB TART

SERVES 6–8

PASTRY

100 g (3½ oz) unsalted butter

55 g (2 oz/¼ cup) caster (superfine) sugar

200 g (7 oz/1⅔ cups) plain (all-purpose) flour

1 egg, lightly beaten

FILLING

100 ml (3½ fl oz) milk

125 ml (4 fl oz/½ cup) pouring cream

1 teaspoon natural vanilla extract

2 x 5 cm (¾ x 2 inch) piece lemon zest, white pith removed

6 egg yolks

55 g (2 oz/¼ cup) caster (superfine) sugar

2 teaspoons plain (all-purpose) flour

300 g (10½ oz) rhubarb, cut into 2 cm (¾ inch) lengths

250 g (9 oz/1⅔ cups) small strawberries, hulled

1 To make the pastry, put the butter and sugar in a small processor fitted with the metal blade. Whizz for 30 seconds, or until combined. Add the flour and a pinch of salt and whizz until just combined. Add the egg and whizz for 10 seconds. With the motor running, add 1 teaspoon of cold water at a time until the dough clumps together. Turn out onto a floured surface. Knead until smooth. Form into a ball, flatten slightly, cover with plastic wrap and chill for 30 minutes.

2 Preheat the oven to 200°C (400°F/Gas 6). Grease a 30 cm (12 inch) loose-based tart tin. Roll out the pastry between two sheets of baking paper until it is 4 mm (⅛ inch) thick and use it to line the prepared tin. Trim the excess pastry, leaving 5 mm (¼ inch) above the tin. Prick base with a fork, line with a piece of crumpled baking paper and pour in some baking beads or uncooked rice. Bake for 15 minutes, then remove the paper

and beads and return to the oven for another 8 minutes, or until lightly golden. Reduce the oven to 180°C (350°F/Gas 4). Place a baking tray on the centre rack.

3 To make the filling, put the milk, cream, vanilla and lemon zest in a heavy-based saucepan. Gently heat over low heat for 8 minutes, or until just below boiling point. Remove from heat and set aside to infuse for 10 minutes. Discard the lemon zest.

4 Place egg yolks, sugar and flour in the cleaned processor. With the motor running, gradually add the infused milk and whizz until the custard is smooth. Pour into prepared pastry case and arrange the rhubarb and strawberries over the top.

5 Put the tart on the baking tray in the oven and bake for 35–40 minutes, or until set. Check the tart after 20 minutes and place a sheet of foil over the top if it is browning too quickly. Serve warm or at room temperature.

SWEET RICOTTA TARTS WITH WALNUT CRUST

SERVES 4

CRUST

200 g (7 oz/2 cups) golden walnuts

3 teaspoons plain (all-purpose) flour

2 tablespoons raw or golden caster (superfine) sugar

40 g (1½ oz) butter, melted

FILLING

300 g (10½ oz/1¼ cups) ricotta cheese

125 g (4½ oz/½ cup) raw or golden caster (superfine) sugar

120 g (4¼ oz/½ cup) crème fraîche or sour cream

2 eggs

30 g (1 oz/¼ cup) plain (all-purpose) flour

1 teaspoon natural vanilla extract

2 teaspoons lemon juice

1 Preheat the oven to 170°C (325°F/Gas 3). Grease four 10.5 cm (4 inch) diameter, 2.5 cm (1 inch) deep loose-based tart tins and line the bases with baking paper.

2 To make the crust, put the walnuts, flour and sugar in a small processor fitted with the metal blade. Whizz in 5-second bursts for 25 seconds, or until fine (whizzing may bring out the oil in the walnuts, causing them to clump).

3 Remove 3 tablespoons of the walnut mixture. Toss half around the insides of the prepared tins to coat them lightly. Reserve the remainder.

4 Add the butter to the processor and whizz for 10 seconds, or until combined with the walnut mixture. Divide the crust among the prepared tins and press firmly over the bases. Put on a baking tray and bake for 10 minutes. Set aside to cool.

5 Meanwhile, to make the filling, add the ricotta and sugar to the cleaned processor and whizz for 15 seconds, or until smooth. Add the crème fraîche or sour cream, eggs, flour, vanilla and lemon juice and whizz until just combined. Divide the filling among the tins, levelling the surface. Put the tins on the baking tray and bake for 15–18 minutes, or until set.

6 Cool the tarts in the tins before turning out. Cover the top of each tart with two strips of paper and, using the reserved walnut mixture, dust two parallel lines over the surface.

MASCARPONE TART WITH BLUEBERRIES

SERVES 4–6

PASTRY

185 g (6½ oz/1½ cups) plain (all-purpose) flour

2 tablespoons caster (superfine) sugar

1 teaspoon finely grated lemon zest

90 g (3¼ oz/⅓ cup) sour cream

2–3 tablespoons light olive oil

250 g (9 oz/1¼ cups) mascarpone cheese

60 g (2¼ oz/¼ cup) sour cream

165 g (5¾ oz/¾ cup) raw or golden caster (superfine) sugar

½ teaspoon finely grated lemon zest

1 teaspoon natural vanilla extract

2 tablespoons cornflour (cornstarch)

4 egg yolks

100 g (3½ oz/⅔ cup) blueberries

icing (confectioners') sugar, to serve

1 **To make the pastry,** put the flour, sugar, lemon zest, sour cream and a large pinch of salt in a small processor fitted with the plastic blade. Whizz for 8–10 seconds, or until combined. With the motor running, gradually add the olive oil, stopping once the mixture resembles wet breadcrumbs. Remove from the processor and knead briefly to form a smooth ball. Cover with plastic wrap and chill for 30 minutes.

2 **Preheat the oven** to 190°C (375°F/Gas 5). Grease an 18 cm (7 inch) loose-based tart tin. Roll out the pastry between two sheets of baking paper to a circle large enough to fit the prepared tin. Use the pastry to line the tin, then trim the edges. Line pastry with a piece of crumpled baking paper and pour in some baking beads or uncooked rice. Bake for 12 minutes, then remove the paper and beads and return to the oven for 8 minutes, or until golden. Set aside to cool for 10 minutes.

3 **Meanwhile,** put the mascarpone, sour cream and sugar in the cleaned processor. Whizz for 15–20 seconds, or until smooth. Add the lemon zest, vanilla, cornflour and egg yolks and whizz for 12–15 seconds, or until combined.

4 **Transfer the mixture** to a metal bowl over a saucepan of simmering water. Cook, stirring often, for 30 minutes, or until the mixture is thickened and holds its shape. Spoon into the pastry case and level the surface. Sprinkle the blueberries over the surface, pressing them in gently. Set aside to cool completely. Serve dusted with icing sugar.

SWEET PUMPKIN PIE

SERVES 8–10

PASTRY

185 g (6½ oz/1½ cups) plain (all-purpose) flour

125 g (4½ oz) unsalted butter, chilled and cubed

3 teaspoons sugar

1 teaspoon finely grated orange zest

1 egg yolk

---

700 g (1 lb 9 oz) jap (kent) pumpkin (squash), peeled, seeded and cubed

80 ml (2½ fl oz/⅓ cup) pouring cream

1 teaspoon ground cinnamon

½ teaspoon ground ginger

½ teaspoon mixed (pumpkin pie) spice

1–2 tablespoons maple syrup

2 tablespoons soft brown sugar

2 eggs

mixed (pumpkin pie) spice, to serve

thick (double/heavy) cream, to serve

---

1 **To make the pastry,** place flour, butter, sugar and orange zest in a small processor fitted with the plastic blade. Whizz in 5-second bursts until the mixture resembles breadcrumbs. Add the egg yolk and 2 tablespoons of cold water and process until the dough comes together into a ball. Add more water if needed, a little at a time. Remove from the processor, shape into a disc and cover with plastic wrap. Chill for 30 minutes.

2 **Put the pumpkin** in a saucepan and cover with water. Bring to the boil, then simmer for 15–20 minutes, or until tender. Drain thoroughly and set aside to cool. You will need 400 g (14 oz/2 cups) of cooked pumpkin. Put the pumpkin in the cleaned processor or a blender and add the cream, cinnamon, ginger, mixed spice, maple syrup, sugar and eggs. Whizz for 30–40 seconds, or until finely puréed.

3 **Preheat the oven** to 200°C (400°F/Gas 6). Grease a 23 cm (9 inch) loose-based flan tin. Roll out the pastry between two sheets of baking paper to a circle large enough to fit the prepared tin. Use the pastry to line the tin. Line the pastry with a piece of crumpled baking paper and pour in some baking beads or uncooked rice. Bake for 10 minutes, then remove the paper and beads and return to the oven for another 10 minutes, or until golden. Set aside to cool for 5 minutes. Reduce the oven to 180°C (350°F/Gas 4). Place a baking tray on the centre rack.

4 **Pour the filling** into the pastry shell. Put the pie on the baking tray in the oven and bake for 40–45 minutes, or until set.

5 **Serve** warm or at room temperature, with cream. Sprinkle with mixed spice.

RED WINE AND CURRANT TART

SERVES 8

200 g (7 oz/1⅓ cups) currants

200 ml (7 fl oz) red wine

200 ml (7 fl oz) blackcurrant juice

½ teaspoon lemon juice

1 cinnamon stick

2 cloves

1 quantity sweet shortcrust pastry
(see page 156)

6 eggs

100 g (3½ oz) caster (superfine) sugar

20 g (¾ oz) butter, melted

icing (confectioners') sugar, for dusting

1 Preheat the oven to 200°C (400°F/Gas 6). Lightly grease a 28 cm (11¼ inch) loose-based round tart tin.

2 Put the currants in a heatproof bowl and set aside. Place red wine, blackcurrant juice, lemon juice, cinnamon and cloves in a saucepan over medium heat. Bring to a simmer. Remove the red wine mixture from the heat and strain the mixture onto the currants in the bowl. Leave the currants to soak in the liquid for 2 hours.

3 Roll out the pastry on a lightly floured work surface until 3 mm (⅛ inch) thick, to fit the base and side of the tart tin. Roll the pastry around the pin, lift and ease into the tin, gently pressing the side to fit, then trim the edges. Wrap the whole tin in plastic wrap and chill in the refrigerator for 1 hour.

4 Line the pastry shell with a crumpled piece of baking paper and cover the base with baking beads or uncooked rice. Bake the pastry for 10 minutes, then remove the paper and beads and bake for a further 8–10 minutes, or until the pastry is golden. Reduce the oven to 160°C (315°F/Gas 2–3).

5 Whisk the eggs with the sugar and butter in a bowl to combine well. Put the currant mixture in a saucepan and warm through, but do not allow it to boil. Pour the warm currant mixture over the egg mixture, stirring to combine. Pour into the tart base. Bake for 30–40 minutes, or until the filling is just set. Allow to cool a little. Serve lightly dusted with icing sugar.

FREEFORM APPLE AND CHERRY CROSTADE

20 g (¾ oz) butter

3 green apples, peeled, cored and cut into 1 cm (½ inch) pieces

60 g (2¼ oz/⅓ cup) soft brown sugar

½ teaspoon ground cinnamon

½ teaspoon ground ginger

½ teaspoon lemon juice

2 tablespoons plain (all-purpose) flour

300 g (10½ oz/2 cups) pitted fresh, frozen or drained tinned cherries

1 quantity sweet shortcrust pastry (see page 156)

1 egg yolk

1 tablespoon milk

JAM GLAZE

80 g (2¾ oz/¼ cup) apricot jam

1½ tablespoons water

1 **Preheat the oven** to 180°C (350°F/Gas 4). Grease and flour a large baking tray.

2 **Melt the butter** in a saucepan over medium heat. Add the apples, brown sugar, cinnamon, ginger and lemon juice and cook, covered, for 5 minutes, or until the apples have softened a little. Remove from the heat, cool a little, then stir in the flour and cherries.

3 **Roll out the pastry** on a lightly floured work surface into a round 3 mm (⅛ inch) thick and place onto the prepared baking tray. Pile the apple and cherry filling into the centre of pastry, leaving a 5 cm (2 inch) border. Fold the pastry over the filling, leaving the centre uncovered, pleating the pastry to fit.

4 **Combine the egg yolk** and milk to make a glaze and brush over the edges of the pastry. Bake the crostade on the bottom shelf of the oven for 35–40 minutes, or until golden.

5 **To make a jam glaze,** combine the apricot jam and 1½ tablespoons water in a small saucepan and bring to a simmer, stirring to combine. Brush the glaze over the pastry and fruit. Let the crostade cool slightly before serving.

PINK GRAPEFRUIT MERINGUE TARTLETS

MAKES 8

2 quantities sweet shortcrust pastry
(see page 156)

GRAPEFRUIT CURD

100 g (3½ oz) butter, chopped

6 eggs, lightly beaten

250 ml (9 fl oz/1 cup) ruby
grapefruit juice

1 tablespoon finely grated ruby
grapefruit zest

170 g (6 oz/¾ cup) caster (superfine)
sugar

MERINGUE

4 egg whites, at room temperature

115 g (4 oz/½ cup) caster (superfine)
sugar

1 tablespoon cornflour (cornstarch)

1 **Preheat the oven** to 180°C (350°F/Gas 4). Lightly grease eight loose-based tartlet tins, 10 cm (4 inches) in diameter and 3 cm (1¼ inches) deep.

2 **Roll out the pastry** on a lightly floured work surface to 3 mm (⅛ inch) thick. Cut the pastry into rounds to fit the base and sides of the tins. Gently press the sides to fit, trim the edges, then wrap the tins in plastic wrap and refrigerate for 30 minutes.

3 **Line each** of the pastry shells with a crumpled piece of baking paper and fill with baking beads or uncooked rice. Blind bake the pastry for 10 minutes, then remove the paper and beads and bake for a further 5 minutes, or until the pastry is golden. Allow to cool.

4 **To make the grapefruit curd,** combine the butter, eggs, grapefruit juice, zest and sugar in a heatproof bowl. Place over a saucepan of simmering water and whisk constantly for 10–15 minutes, or until the mixture thickens. Set aside to cool.

Spoon the curd into the tart shells, smoothing the top. Place in the refrigerator for 30 minutes, or until completely cold.

5 **To make the meringue,** whisk the egg whites in a clean, dry bowl until soft peaks form. Add the sugar, 1 tablespoon at a time, whisking well after each addition. Whisk until the mixture is stiff and glossy and the sugar has dissolved. Add cornflour, whisking to mix well.

6 **Place the mixture** in a piping bag fitted with a 2 cm (¾ inch) plain nozzle. Remove tartlets from the refrigerator and pipe the meringue over the curd. Bake for 10 minutes, or until the meringue is golden.

Note: Pastry is baked blind to ensure that the finished pastry is crisp, whatever type of filling it contains.

APPLE AND AMARETTI PIE

SERVES 8–10

2 quantities sweet shortcrust pastry (see page 156)

40 g (1½ oz) butter

5 green apples, peeled, cored and thinly sliced

1 teaspoon lemon juice

½ teaspoon ground cinnamon

80 g (2¾ oz/⅓ cup) soft brown sugar

25 g (1 oz/¼ cup) flaked almonds, toasted

50 g (1¾ oz/1 cup) roughly chopped amaretti

1 egg yolk

icing (confectioners') sugar, for dusting

1 **Preheat the oven** to 200°C (400°F/Gas 6). Grease a 23 x 3 cm (9 x 1¼ inch) pie dish.

2 **Using two-thirds of the pastry,** roll it out on a lightly floured work surface until 3 mm (⅛ inch) thick, to fit the base and side of the dish. Roll the pastry around the pin, then lift and ease it into the dish. Trim the edges, cover with plastic wrap and refrigerate for 30 minutes. Roll out the remaining pastry until 3 mm (⅛ inch) thick, to fit the top of the dish. Put the pastry round onto a large plate, cover with plastic wrap and refrigerate for 30 minutes.

3 **Line the pastry shell** with crumpled baking paper and cover the base with baking beads or uncooked rice. Bake for 10 minutes, then remove the paper and beads and bake for a further 10 minutes, or until pastry is golden. Remove from the oven. Reduce the temperature to 180°C (350°F/Gas 4).

4 **Melt the butter** in a large saucepan. Add the apples, lemon juice, cinnamon and brown sugar and cook, covered, over medium heat for 5 minutes, or until the apple begins to soften. Remove from the heat and stir in the almonds and amaretti.

5 **Spoon the mixture** into the pastry shell. Combine the egg yolk with 1 tablespoon water and brush over the edge of the pastry. Cover with the pastry round, gently pressing the pastry together to seal the edges. Cut a small hole in the centre to allow steam to escape and brush the top with the egg wash. Bake for 45 minutes, or until the pastry is golden. Cool, then lightly dust with icing sugar to serve.

Note: Amaretti are a light crisp Italian macaroon biscuit made with sweet and bitter almonds.

CROQUEMBOUCHE WITH COFFEE CREAM FILLING

SERVES 10

1 quantity choux pastry (see page 157), made into 40 choux puffs, cooled

COFFEE CREAM FILLING

1½ tablespoons instant coffee granules

400 g (14 oz) mascarpone

60 g (2¼ oz/½ cup) icing (confectioners') sugar

2 tablespoons pouring cream

CARAMEL

700 g (1 lb 9 oz/3 cups) caster (superfine) sugar

250 ml (9 fl oz/1 cup) water

1 **To make the coffee cream filling,** dissolve the coffee in 1 tablespoon boiling water. Place in a bowl with mascarpone, icing sugar and cream Mix well, using electric beaters.

2 **Place the filling** in a piping bag fitted with a nozzle less than 1 cm (½ inch) in diameter. Using the end of a teaspoon, make a small hole in the base of each choux puff, then pipe the filling into the puffs.

3 **To make caramel,** put the sugar and 250 ml (9 fl oz/1 cup) water in a heavy-based saucepan. Slowly bring to a simmer over medium heat. Cook, without stirring, for 20 minutes, or until the mixture turns a deep caramel colour. Remove from the heat and immediately put the saucepan into a large bowl of cold water to stop the caramel cooking further.

4 **To assemble,** dip the base of three puffs into the caramel and place them on a serving plate to form a triangular shape.

Dip the base of a fourth puff into the caramel and place on top of the triangle, in the centre, to form a small pyramid. Repeat to make 10 individual pyramids in total.

5 **Dip two forks** into the remaining caramel, then rub the backs of the forks together until the caramel begins to stick. Gently pull the forks apart to check whether the caramel is cool enough to spin. If it drips, it probably needs longer to cool. When the caramel forms fine threads of toffee, spin it around each croquembouche until they are covered with fine threads of toffee. Serve immediately.

Note: Croquembouche, meaning 'crunch in the mouth', is a traditional French dessert often served at weddings. You can assemble the puffs to make one large croquembouche. Start with a large circle of puffs at the base (an odd number works best) and gradually build up layers to form a pyramid shape.

GREAT TASTES DESSERTS

ESPRESSO CHOCOLATE TART

SERVES 12

1 quantity sweet shortcrust pastry (see page 156), made with 2 tablespoons finely ground coffee beans substituted for 2 tablespoons of the flour

50 g (1¾ oz/⅓ cup) dark chocolate, chopped

400 g (14 oz/2⅔ cups) milk chocolate, chopped

300 ml (10½ fl oz) thick (double/heavy) cream

1 **Preheat the oven** to 200°C (400°F/Gas 6). Grease a 35 x 11 cm (14 x 4¼ inch) loose-based rectangular shallow tart tin.

2 **Roll out pastry** on a lightly floured work surface until 3 mm (⅛ inch) thick, to fit the base and sides of the tin. Roll the pastry around the pin, then lift and ease it into the tin, gently pressing to fit into the corners. Trim the edges, cover with plastic wrap and refrigerate for 1 hour.

3 **Line the pastry shell** with crumpled baking paper and cover the base with baking beads or uncooked rice. Bake the pastry for 10 minutes, then remove the paper and beads and bake for a further 10 minutes, or until the pastry is golden.

4 **Put the dark chocolate** in a small heatproof bowl. Sit the bowl over a small saucepan of simmering water, stirring frequently until the chocolate has melted and the mixture is smooth. Take care that the base of the bowl doesn't touch the water. Brush the base of the pastry with melted chocolate.

5 **Put the milk chocolate** and cream in a small heatproof bowl. Sit the bowl over a small saucepan of simmering water, stirring until the chocolate has melted and the mixture is smooth. Allow the chocolate to cool slightly, then pour into the tart case. Refrigerate overnight, or until the filling has set. Serve the tart in small slices as it is very rich.

PISTACHIO PITHIVIERS

SERVES 10

120 g (4¼ oz) butter, softened

145 g (5½ oz/⅔ cup) caster (superfine) sugar

2 egg yolks

200 g (7 oz/1⅓ cups) pistachios, lightly toasted, then finely ground

½ teaspoon natural vanilla extract

30 g (1 oz/¼ cup) plain (all-purpose) flour

2 sheets frozen butter puff pastry, thawed

1 egg yolk, extra

1 tablespoon milk

2 tablespoons apricot jam

1 tablespoon chopped toasted pistachios

1 **Preheat the oven** to 180°C (350°F/Gas 4). Line a baking tray with baking paper.

2 **Cream the butter** and sugar in a bowl, using electric beaters, until pale and fluffy, then add the yolks one at a time, beating well after each addition. Stir in the ground pistachios, vanilla and flour.

3 **Cut the puff pastry** into two 24 cm (9½ inch) rounds. Place one round onto the prepared baking tray. Spoon the pistachio mixture into the middle of the pastry, smoothing the surface, leaving a 4 cm (1½ inch) border around the edge. Combine the extra egg yolk and milk in a small bowl. Lightly brush around the border with the egg mixture, then top with the remaining pastry round. Press the edges together to seal, then use your fingertips to crimp the edge at 2 cm (¾ inch) intervals. Using the back of a small knife, score the pastry into

wedges, starting from the centre and working out towards the edge (take care not to cut all the way through the pastry). Brush the surface with the remaining egg mixture. Bake on the bottom oven shelf for 45 minutes, or until golden and puffed.

4 **Heat the jam** in a small saucepan with 1 tablespoon water. As soon as the pithiviers comes out of the oven, brush liberally with the apricot glaze, then sprinkle with the chopped pistachios. Allow to cool, then serve. Eat the day it is made.

Note: Toasted nuts can be ground in a food processor. Place the cooled nuts in the bowl and, using the pulse button, process in short bursts until the nuts resemble breadcrumbs; do not overprocess or the nuts will become oily. If the recipe uses sugar, it helps to add a little to the nuts when processing to help absorb some of the oil.

PEAR TARTE TATIN

SERVES 8

145 g (5 oz/⅔ cup) caster (superfine) sugar
50 g (1¾ oz) butter, chopped
½ teaspoon ground ginger
½ teaspoon ground cinnamon
3 beurre bosc pears, peeled, cored and cut into wedges
450 g (1 lb) block frozen butter puff pastry, thawed
thick (double/heavy) cream, to serve

1 Preheat the oven to 220°C (425°F/Gas 7). Put a 22 cm (8½ inch) heavy-based frying pan with an ovenproof handle over medium heat. Add the sugar and heat, shaking the pan constantly, until the sugar is a dark caramel colour. Add butter, ginger and cinnamon and stir to combine. Arrange the pears on top, spoon over the caramel to coat, then reduce the heat to low and cook, covered, for 5 minutes, or until the pears just begin to soften.

2 Remove the frying pan from the heat and arrange the pears over the base of the pan, overlapping them neatly to make a decorative finish when the tart is turned out. Leave to cool slightly.

3 Roll out the pastry on a lightly floured work surface to a 24 cm (9½ inch) round. Place the pastry over the pears in the frying pan, tucking the edges around the pears so they are enclosed in pastry. Bake for 20–25 minutes, or until the pastry is golden and puffed. Leave for 10 minutes, then run a knife around the edge of the pan to loosen the tart and invert onto a serving platter. Serve warm with cream. The tart is best served on the day it is made.

Note: A cast-iron frying pan with an ovenproof handle works best for this tart, but you can use any heavy-based frying pan, as long as it is ovenproof.

COCOA AND DATE CROSTATA

SERVES 12

500 g (1 lb 2 oz/2¾ cups) pitted dried dates

½ teaspoon natural vanilla extract

2 teaspoons lemon zest

½ teaspoon ground cinnamon

½ teaspoon ground ginger

30 g (1 oz/¼ cup) unsweetened cocoa powder

1 tablespoon soft brown sugar

¼ teaspoon bicarbonate of soda (baking soda)

1½ quantities sweet shortcrust pastry (see page 156), but substitute 75 g (2½ oz) toasted walnuts, blended until fine, for 75 g (2½ oz) of the flour

1 egg yolk

1 teaspoon caster (superfine) sugar

¼ teaspoon ground cinnamon, extra

1 **Preheat the oven** to 180°C (350°F/Gas 4). Put the dates, vanilla, lemon zest, cinnamon, ginger, cocoa powder, brown sugar and 250 ml (9 fl oz/1 cup) water in a heavy-based saucepan over medium heat. Bring to a simmer, then add the bicarbonate of soda, stir to combine and set aside to cool. Transfer the mixture to a food processor and, using the pulse button, mix to form a coarse paste.

2 **Grease a deep,** 25 cm (10 inch) loose-based round tart tin. Using two-thirds of the pastry, roll out the pastry to fit the base and side of the tin. Roll out the remaining pastry to form a round, large enough for the top.

3 **Spoon the filling** over the pastry, smoothing the top. Combine the egg yolk with 1 tablespoon water and brush the edges with the egg wash. Place the pastry round over the date filling, gently pressing to remove any air bubbles, and pressing the edges of the pastry together to seal. Cut a slit in the middle of the pastry to allow the steam to escape, then brush the top with the remaining egg wash. Sprinkle with the cinnamon mix.

4 **Place on the bottom shelf** of the oven and bake for 1 hour, or until golden. Cool completely before serving.

PANNA COTTA FILO WITH ROSEWATER SYRUP

SERVES 6

PANNA COTTA

1 x 6 g (1/8 oz) gelatine sheet (or
    1½ teaspoons powdered gelatine)

500 ml (17 fl oz/2 cups) thick (double/
    heavy) cream

250 g (9 oz/1 cup) plain yoghurt

150 g (5½ oz/2/3 cup) caster (superfine)
    sugar

1 vanilla bean

FILO SHELLS

4 sheets filo pastry

40 g (1½ oz) unsalted butter
    melted

2 tablespoons caster (superfine) sugar

ROSEWATER SYRUP

115 g (4 oz/½ cup) caster (superfine)
    sugar

1 cinnamon stick

½ teaspoon rosewater

1 drop rose pink food colouring
    (optional)

2 tablespoons roasted pistachio nuts,
    chopped, to serve

1 **To make the panna cotta,** either soak the gelatine sheet in cold water for 5 minutes, or until soft, or put 2 tablespoons of water in a small bowl, sprinkle with the powdered gelatine and set aside for 2 minutes to swell. Put the cream, yoghurt and sugar in a saucepan. Split the vanilla bean lengthways and scrape the seeds into the saucepan, discarding the pod. Stir the mixture over low heat until the sugar has dissolved. Drain the gelatine sheet and squeeze out excess water. Add the gelatine sheet or the sponged gelatine to the saucepan and stir until the gelatine has dissolved. Pour the mixture into 6 x 125 ml (4 fl oz/½ cup) ramekins. Refrigerate for 5 hours, or until set.

2 **Preheat the oven** to 190°C (375°F/Gas 5). Lightly brush a sheet of filo pastry with the melted butter. Sprinkle one-third of the sugar over the pastry, top with another sheet of pastry and press down gently to stick the pastry together. Repeat this process until there are four layers of pastry. Using a sharp knife, cut 6 x 12 cm (4½ inch) square pieces from the pastry. Line a 6-hole giant muffin tin with the pastry squares. Line each pastry shell with a square of baking paper and weigh it down with baking beads or uncooked rice. Bake for 2 minutes, then remove the paper and beads and bake a further 2–3 minutes, or until lightly golden. Cool the pastry shells on a wire rack.

3 **To make rosewater syrup,** put 160 ml (5¼ fl oz) of water, the sugar and cinnamon stick in a small saucepan. Stir over low heat until sugar has dissolved. Increase heat to high. Simmer for 4 minutes, or until mixture is slightly syrupy. Add rosewater and food colouring. Set aside to cool. Discard cinnamon stick.

4 **Run a spatula** around the panna cotta, then carefully invert into the pastry shells. Drizzle with rosewater syrup and sprinkle with the pistachios.

LEMON TART

SERVES 6–8

PASTRY

185 g (6½ oz/1½ cups) plain (all-purpose) flour

60 g (2¼ oz/½ cup) icing (confectioners') sugar

35 g (1¼ oz/⅓ cup) ground almonds

125 g (4½ oz) unsalted butter, chilled and cubed

1 egg yolk, at room temperature

FILLING

1½ tablespoons lemon zest finely grated

80 ml (2½ fl oz/⅓ cup) lemon juice, strained

5 eggs, at room temperature

175 g (6 oz/¾ cup) caster (superfine) sugar

300 ml (10½ fl oz) thick (double/heavy) cream

icing (confectioners') sugar, for dusting

thick (double/heavy) cream, to serve

1 **To make the pastry,** put the flour, icing sugar, ground almonds and butter in a food processor and process until the mixture resembles fine crumbs. Add the egg yolk and process until the dough just comes together. Knead gently and briefly on a lightly floured surface until the dough is smooth. Form into a ball, flatten into a disc, cover with plastic wrap and refrigerate for 30 minutes.

2 **Preheat the oven** to 180°C (350°F/Gas 4). Grease a 22 cm (8½ inch) loose-based tart tin. Roll out the pastry between two sheets of baking paper to a thickness of 3 mm (⅛ inch) to cover the base and side of the tart tin. Peel off the top sheet of baking paper, carefully invert the pastry into the tin and peel off the second sheet of paper. Press the pastry gently into the base and side, ensuring the pastry is level with the top of the tin. Trim off any excess pastry. Refrigerate for 10 minutes.

3 **Line the pastry** with a sheet of crumpled baking paper and pour in some baking beads or uncooked rice. Place the tin on a baking tray and bake for 10 minutes. Remove the paper and beads and return to the oven for another 10–15 minutes, or until light golden. Set aside to cool. Reduce the oven to 140°C (275°F/Gas 1).

4 **To make the filling,** put the lemon zest, lemon juice, eggs, sugar and cream in a bowl and whisk until combined. Set aside for 10 minutes to allow the lemon zest to infuse the mixture, then strain the mixture. Carefully pour the filling into the pastry shell and bake for 45–50 minutes, or until just set. Set aside to cool for 10 minutes, then refrigerate until cold.

5 **Dust the tart** with icing sugar and serve with thick cream.

COCONUT, MANGO AND ALMOND TART

SERVES 6–8

PASTRY

210 g (7½ oz/1⅔ cups) plain (all-purpose) flour

60 g (2¼ oz/¼ cup) raw caster (superfine) sugar

25 g (1 oz/¼ cup) ground almonds

150 g (5½ oz) unsalted butter, chilled and cubed

2 egg yolks, at room temperature

1–2 tablespoons iced water

FILLING

185 g (6½ oz) unsalted butter, softened

185 g (6½ oz/heaped ¾ cup) raw caster (superfine) sugar

2 eggs, at room temperature

70 g (2½ oz/⅔ cup) ground almonds

60 g (2¼ oz/½ cup) plain (all-purpose) flour

90 g (3¼ oz/1 cup) desiccated coconut

2 tablespoons coconut cream

1 tablespoon coconut liqueur

1 mango

30 g (1 oz/½ cup) flaked coconut

vanilla ice cream or whipped cream, to serve

1 **To make the pastry,** put the flour, sugar, ground almonds and butter in a food processor. Process until mixture resembles fine crumbs. Add egg yolks and process until smooth. Add the water, ½ teaspoon at a time, until the dough clumps together in a ball. Flatten the dough to a rough rectangle, cover with plastic wrap and refrigerate for 30 minutes.

2 **Preheat the oven** to 190°C (375°F/Gas 5) and grease a 19 x 27 cm (7½ x 10¾ inch) loose-based tart tin.

3 **To make the filling,** cream the butter and sugar with electric beaters for about 3 minutes. Add the eggs, one at a time, beating well after each addition. Fold in the ground almonds, flour and desiccated coconut. Lightly stir in the coconut cream and coconut liqueur.

4 **Roll out the pastry** on a sheet of baking paper to cover the base and side of the tin. Place the pastry in the tin and trim any excess. Line pastry with crumpled baking paper and pour in some baking beads or uncooked rice. Bake 10 minutes, remove the paper and beads and bake for another 5 minutes. Reduce the oven to 170°C (325°F/Gas 3).

5 **Slice cheeks from the mango,** peel them and cut each into 3 mm (⅛ inch) thick slices. Spread the filling in the pastry case and arrange mango slices in two rows down the length of the filling. Scatter the flaked coconut over the top and press it into the exposed filling with your fingertips, giving an uneven surface. Bake for 30 minutes, or until coconut starts to brown, then cover loosely with foil. Bake for another 35 minutes, or until the filling is set and the top is golden brown. Serve warm with vanilla ice cream or serve cold with whipped cream.

NECTARINE PUFF PASTRIES

MAKES 8

2 sheets frozen butter puff pastry, thawed

50 g (1¾ oz) unsalted butter, softened

55 g (2 oz/½ cup) ground almonds

½ teaspoon natural vanilla extract

5 large nectarines

55 g (2 oz/¼ cup) caster (superfine) sugar

110 g (3¾ oz/⅓ cup) apricot or peach jam, warmed and sieved

1 **Preheat the oven** to 200°C (400°F/Gas 6). Line two large baking trays with baking paper.

2 **Cut the pastry sheets** into 8 x 12 cm (4½ inch) rounds and place on the prepared trays. Combine the butter, ground almonds and vanilla in a small bowl to form a paste. Divide the paste among the pastry rounds and spread evenly, leaving a 1.5 cm (⅝ inch) border around the edge.

3 **Halve the nectarines,** removing the stones, and cut them into 5 mm (¼ inch) slices. Arrange the nectarine slices over the pastry rounds, overlapping the slices and leaving a thin border. Sprinkle sugar over the nectarines.

4 **Bake for 15 minutes,** or until the pastries are puffed and golden. Brush the nectarines and pastry with the warm jam while the pastries are hot. Serve hot or at room temperature.

CARAMELIZED PEACH AND PASSIONFRUIT CRUMBLE TART

SERVES 6

1 quantity ready-made shortcrust pastry (see page 156)

80 g (2¾ oz/⅔ cup) plain (all-purpose) flour

40 g (1½ oz/¼ cup) soft brown sugar

40 g (1½ oz) unsalted butter, chilled and cubed

20 g (¾ oz/¼ cup) desiccated coconut

2 tablespoons, roasted skinned hazelnuts, chopped

4 peaches, sliced

80 g (2¾ oz/⅓ cup) caster (superfine) sugar

3 passionfruit

1 **Preheat the oven** to 200°C (400°F/Gas 6). Roll out the pastry to cover the base and side of a 20 cm (8 inch), 4 cm (1½ inch) deep flan tin. Place the pastry in the tin and prick the base. Line the pastry shell with a sheet of crumpled baking paper and pour in some baking beads or uncooked rice. Bake for 15 minutes, then remove the paper and beads and return to the oven for another 6–8 minutes. Set aside to cool. Reduce the oven to 180°C (350°F/Gas 4).

2 **Rub the flour,** brown sugar and butter together. Add the coconut and chopped hazelnuts. Set aside.

3 **Heat a frying pan** over high heat. Toss the peach slices in the caster sugar. Tip the peaches into the frying pan and cook, moving them occasionally until they are evenly coated in caramel. Add the passionfruit pulp and remove the pan from the heat.

4 **Spoon the peach mixture** into the pastry case and top with the hazelnut mixture. Bake the tart for 20–25 minutes, or until the top is golden brown.

BLACKBERRY AND PEAR STRUDEL

SERVES 4

120 g (4¼ oz) unsalted butter

½ teaspoon natural vanilla extract

4 pears, peeled, cored and chopped

1 teaspoon orange zest, finely grated

½ lemon, juiced

5 sheets filo pastry

120 g (4¼ oz/1½ cups) fresh breadcrumbs

200 g (7 oz/1½ cups) blackberries

50 g (1¾ oz/½ cup) toasted flaked almonds

60 g (2¼ oz/½ cup) sultanas

165 g (5¾ oz/¾ cup) caster (superfine) sugar

icing (confectioners') sugar for dusting

custard or vanilla ice cream, to serve

1 **Preheat the oven** to 180°C (350°F/Gas 4) and line a baking sheet with baking paper. Melt 100 g (3½ oz) of the butter with the vanilla.

2 **Melt the remaining butter** in a frying pan and sauté the pear over low heat for 5 minutes, or until tender. Transfer to a large bowl with the orange zest and lemon juice. Toss lightly to combine.

3 **Lay a sheet of filo pastry** on a flat surface. Brush melted butter over the pastry and sprinkle lightly with breadcrumbs. Cover with another sheet of pastry and repeat the process until you have used all the pastry, then sprinkle with the remaining breadcrumbs.

4 **Add blackberries, almonds,** sultanas and caster sugar to the pear mixture and toss gently to combine. Shape the filling into a log along one long edge of the pastry, leaving a 5 cm (2 inch) border. Fold in the sides, then roll up and place, seam side down, on the prepared baking sheet. Brush with the remaining melted butter and bake for 40 minutes, or until golden brown. Dust with icing sugar and serve with custard or vanilla ice cream.

PLUM AND ALMOND TART

SERVES 8

PASTRY

185 g (6½ oz/1½ cups) plain (all-purpose) flour

150 g (5½ oz) unsalted butter, chilled and cubed

55 g (2 oz/¼ cup) caster (superfine) sugar

1 tablespoon sour cream

FILLING

125 g (4½ oz) unsalted butter, softened

115 g (4 oz/½ cup) caster (superfine) sugar

2 eggs, at room temperature

100 g (3½ oz/1 cup) ground almonds

2 tablespoons plain (all-purpose) flour

8–10 plums, halved, stones removed

cream or ice cream, to serve

1 To make the pastry, put the flour, butter and sugar in a food processor and process in short bursts until the mixture resembles fine breadcrumbs. Add the sour cream and process in short bursts until the mixture comes together in a ball. Cover with plastic wrap and refrigerate for 20 minutes.

2 Preheat the oven to 200°C (400°F/Gas 6) and grease a 23 cm (9 inch), 2 cm (¾ inch) deep loose-based flan tin.

3 Roll out the pastry to a thickness of 3 mm (⅛ inch) and use it to line the tin. Prick the pastry base with a fork and refrigerate for 30 minutes. Line the pastry shell with a sheet of crumpled baking paper and pour in some baking beads or uncooked rice. Bake for 15 minutes, remove the paper and beads and return to the oven for another 5–7 minutes to ensure the pastry is crisp. Set aside to cool. Reduce the oven to 180°C (350°F/Gas 4).

4 To make the filling, cream the butter and sugar with electric beaters until light and fluffy. Add the eggs, one at a time, beating well after each addition. Fold in the ground almonds and flour. Spread the almond mixture over the base of the pastry case and top with the plum halves, cut side down. Bake for 25–30 minutes, or until the filling is set and golden. Serve the tart warm or at room temperature with cream or ice cream.

BAKED YOGHURT TART WITH FIGS AND HAZELNUTS

SERVES 6–8

PASTRY

150 g (5½ oz/1¼ cups) plain (all-purpose) flour

80 g (2¾ oz/¾ cup) ground hazelnuts

90 g (3¼ oz) unsalted butter, cubed

1 egg yolk, at room temperature

FILLING

3 eggs, at room temperature

2 egg yolks, at room temperature

125 g (4½ oz/heaped ½ cup) caster (superfine) sugar

2 vanilla beans, split lengthways

200 g (7 oz/heaped ¾ cup) Greek-style yoghurt

30 g (1 oz/¼ cup) cornflour (cornstarch)

30 g (1 oz/¼ cup) plain (all-purpose) flour

7 figs, sliced

100 g (3½ oz/heaped ¾ cup) roasted skinned hazelnuts, roughly chopped

whipped cream, to serve

1 To make the pastry, put the flour, ground hazelnuts, butter and a pinch of salt in a food processor and process until the mixture resembles breadcrumbs. Add the egg yolk and 1 tablespoon of cold water. Process until the mixture just forms a ball, adding a little extra water if the dough is too dry. Turn out onto a work surface and flatten into a disc. Cover with plastic wrap and refrigerate for 30 minutes.

2 Preheat the oven to 180°C (350°F/Gas 4). Lightly grease a 23 cm (9 inch) shallow tart tin. Roll out the pastry on a lightly floured surface until 3 mm (⅛ inch) thick. Carefully transfer the pastry into the tin, prick the base with a fork and refrigerate for 10 minutes. Roll a rolling pin across the top of the tart tin to remove any excess pastry.

3 To make the filling, beat the eggs, egg yolks and sugar in a bowl until the sugar has dissolved. Scrape the seeds from the vanilla beans into the egg mixture and stir in the yoghurt. Combine the cornflour and plain flour and lightly fold through the yoghurt mixture. Pour into the pastry case and top with the sliced figs and chopped hazelnuts. Bake for 18–20 minutes, or until just set. Leave the tart to cool in the tin, then remove and serve at room temperature. Serve with whipped cream.

CHOCOLATE GANACHE LOG

SERVES 8–10

CAKE

200 g (7 oz) unsalted butter, softened

150 g (5½ oz/⅔ cup) caster (superfine) sugar

6 eggs, at room temperature, separated

125 g (4½ oz/1¼ cups) ground almonds

150 g (5½ oz/1 cup) dark chocolate chopped, melted

GANACHE

150 ml (5 fl oz) thick (double/heavy) cream

225 g (8 oz/1½ cups) dark chocolate chopped

2 teaspoons instant coffee granules

1 To make the cake, preheat the oven to 180°C (350°F/ Gas 4). Grease and line a 25 x 30 cm (10 x 12 inch) Swiss roll tin (jelly roll tin).

2 Beat the butter and sugar with electric beaters until light and fluffy. Add the egg yolks, one at a time, beating well after each addition. Stir in the ground almonds and melted chocolate. Beat the egg whites in a separate bowl until stiff peaks form, then gently fold into the chocolate mixture.

3 Spread the mixture into the prepared tin and bake for 15 minutes. Reduce the oven to 160°C (315°F/Gas 2–3) and bake for another 30 minutes, or until a skewer comes out clean when inserted into the centre of the cake. Turn the cake onto a wire rack to cool.

4 To make the ganache, put the cream and chopped chocolate in a heatproof bowl over a small saucepan of barely simmering water, making sure the base of the bowl doesn't touch the water. Stir occasionally until the mixture is melted and combined. Stir in the coffee until it has dissolved. Remove from the heat and set aside to cool for 2 hours, or until thickened to a spreading consistency.

5 Cut the cake lengthways into three even pieces. Place a piece of cake on a serving plate and spread with a layer of ganache. Top with another layer of cake and another layer of ganache, followed by the remaining cake. Refrigerate for 30 minutes to set slightly. Cover the top and sides of the log with the remaining ganache and refrigerate for 3 hours, or preferably overnight.

PLUM UPSIDE-DOWN CAKE

SERVES 8

450 g (1 lb) plums

30 g (1 oz/¼ cup) dark muscovado
  sugar

100 g (3½ oz) unsalted butter, softened

250 g (9 oz/1 heaped cup) caster
  (superfine) sugar

4 eggs, at room temperature

1 teaspoon natural vanilla extract

1 orange, zest grated

6 cardamom pods, seeds removed and
  crushed

150 g (5½ oz/1¼ cups) plain
  (all-purpose) flour

150 g (5½ oz/1½ cups) ground almonds

baking powder

thick (double/heavy) cream, to serve

1   Preheat the oven to 180°C (350°F/Gas 4). Grease and line a 23 cm (9 inch) spring-form cake tin.

2   Halve the plums and remove stones. Sprinkle muscovado sugar over the base of the prepared tin and arrange the plums, cut side down, over the sugar.

3   Cream the butter and caster sugar with electric beaters until light and fluffy. Add eggs, one at a time, beating well after each addition. Add the vanilla, orange zest, crushed cardamom seeds, flour, ground almonds and baking powder. Spoon over the plums and smooth the surface with a spatula.

4   Bake for 50 minutes, or until a skewer comes out clean when inserted in the centre of the cake. Set aside to cool for 5 minutes before turning the cake out onto a plate. Serve with thick cream.

PEAR DUMPLINGS

SERVES 6

6 firm, ripe pears

100 g (3½ oz) goat's cheese, crumbled

55 g (2 oz/½ cup) ground almonds

½ teaspoon ground nutmeg

½ teaspoon grated lemon zest

55 g (2 oz/¼ cup) caster (superfine) sugar

1½ quantities sweet shortcrust pastry (see page 156)

1 egg, lightly beaten

icing (confectioners') sugar, for dusting

crème anglaise, to serve (see page 51)

1 Preheat the oven to 180°C (350°F/Gas 4). Grease a large roasting tin.

2 Leaving the pears whole and unpeeled, core them using an apple corer. Combine the goat's cheese, almonds, nutmeg, lemon zest and 2 tablespoons of the sugar. Using a teaspoon, fill the pear cavities with the goat's cheese mixture.

3 Roll out the pastry to 3 mm (⅛ inch) thick and cut into six 15 cm (6 inch) squares. Lightly brush the squares with egg and sprinkle with the remaining sugar. Place a pear in the centre of each piece of pastry and bring the corners of the pastry up and around the pear to completely enclose it. Press the edges together to seal, trimming where necessary, and reserving the pastry scraps.

4 Using a small knife, cut 12 leaf shapes from the pastry scraps. Brush the dumplings with the remaining egg and attach two pastry leaves to the top of each, pressing firmly to secure. Transfer to the roasting tin and bake for about 35 minutes, or until the pastry is golden and the pears are tender. Dust with icing sugar and serve immediately with crème anglaise or pouring cream, if preferred.

PUDDINGS

CHOCOLATE FUDGE PUDDINGS

SERVES 8

150 g (5½ oz) unsalted butter

175 g (6 oz/¾ cup) caster (superfine) sugar

100 g (3½ oz) dark chocolate, melted and cooled (see Note)

2 eggs

60 g (2¼ oz/½ cup) plain (all-purpose) flour

90 g (3¼ oz/¾ cup) self-raising flour

30 g (1 oz/¼ cup) unsweetened cocoa powder

1 teaspoon bicarbonate of soda (baking soda)

125 ml (4 fl oz/½ cup) milk

SAUCE

50 g (1¾ oz) unsalted butter, chopped

125 g (4½ oz/1 cup) dark chocolate, chopped

125 ml (4 fl oz/½ cup) thick (double/heavy) cream

1 teaspoon natural vanilla extract

whipped cream, to serve

1 Preheat the oven to 180°C (350°F/Gas 4). Lightly grease eight 250 ml (9 fl oz/1 cup) ramekins or ovenproof tea cups.

2 Using electric beaters, beat the butter and sugar until light and creamy. Add the melted chocolate, beating well. Add the eggs one at a time, beating well after each addition.

3 Sift together the flours, cocoa and bicarbonate of soda, then gently fold into the chocolate mixture. Add the milk and fold through. Half-fill the ramekins, then cover with pieces of greased foil and place in a large, deep roasting tin. Pour in enough hot water to come halfway up the sides of the ramekins. Bake for 35 minutes, or until a skewer inserted in the centre of each pudding comes out clean.

4 To make the sauce, combine the butter, chocolate, cream and vanilla in a saucepan. Stir over low heat until the butter and chocolate have completely melted. Pour sauce over the puddings and serve with whipped cream.

Note: To melt chocolate, cut it into cubes and place in a heatproof bowl. Sit the bowl over a saucepan of simmering water, making sure the water does not touch the base, and stir with a metal spoon until melted.

BLACKBERRY PUDDINGS WITH CREME ANGLAISE

SERVES 8

125 g (4½ oz) unsalted butter, softened

125 g (4½ oz/heaped ½ cup) caster (superfine) sugar

2 eggs, at room temperature

125 g (4½ oz/1 cup) self-raising flour

2 tablespoons milk

250 g (9 oz/2¼ cups) blackberries

CRÈME ANGLAISE

325 ml (11 fl oz) milk

4 egg yolks, at room temperature

80 g (2¾ oz/⅓ cup) caster (superfine) sugar

1 Preheat the oven to 180°C (350°F/Gas 4) and grease eight 125 ml (4 fl oz/½ cup) dariole moulds.

2 Using electric beaters, cream the butter and sugar together until light and fluffy. Add the eggs, one at a time, beating well after each addition. Sift the flour and gently fold in with enough milk to form a dropping consistency.

3 Cover the base of each mould with a layer of blackberries. Spoon enough of the pudding mixture over the berries so that the moulds are three-quarters full. Cover the moulds with foil, sealing tightly. Place puddings in a roasting tin and pour in enough hot water to come halfway up the sides of the moulds. Bake for about 30–35 minutes, or until the puddings spring back when lightly touched.

4 Meanwhile, to make the crème anglaise, heat the milk to just below boiling point, then set aside. Beat the egg yolks and sugar with electric beaters until thick and pale. Slowly whisk in the hot milk and pour the mixture into a saucepan. Cook over low heat, stirring constantly, for 5–7 minutes, or until the custard is thick enough to coat the back of a spoon. Remove from the heat.

5 To serve, unmould the puddings onto plates. Drizzle with the crème anglaise, or serve with pouring cream, if preferred..

COCONUT AND GINGER PUDDINGS WITH LIME SYRUP

SERVES 6

LIME SYRUP

115 g (4 oz/½ cup) caster (superfine)
    sugar

2 makrut (kaffir lime) leaves, crushed

2 tablespoons lime juice

125 g (4½ oz) softened butter

115 g (4 oz/½ cup) caster (superfine)
    sugar

2 eggs

155 g (5½ oz/1¼ cups) self-raising flour

2 teaspoons ground ginger

1 tablespoon chopped glacé ginger

125 ml (4 fl oz/½ cup) coconut milk

whipped cream, to serve

1 **To make the lime syrup,** put the sugar and 125 ml (4 fl oz/ ½ cup) of water in a saucepan and stir over low heat until the sugar has dissolved. Add the lime leaves, bring to the boil and cook for 5–6 minutes, or until thick and syrupy. Stir in the lime juice and leave to cool. When cool, remove the lime leaves.

2 **Lightly grease** six 125 ml (4 fl oz/½ cup) ramekins.

3 **Using electric beaters,** beat the butter and sugar until light and creamy. Add the eggs one at a time, mixing well after each addition. Fold in the sifted flour, ground ginger and glacé ginger alternately with the coconut milk until combined.

4 **Spoon the mixture** into the ramekins, smooth the surface, then arrange in a bamboo steamer. Sit the steamer over a wok of simmering water and steam, covered, for 15 minutes, or until cooked when tested with a skewer.

5 **Cool for 5 minutes,** then run a knife around the puddings and turn out onto serving plates. Drizzle with some syrup and serve with whipped cream.

CHOCOLATE MINT SELF-SAUCING PUDDING

SERVES 6

185 ml (6 fl oz/¾ cup) milk

115 g (4 oz/½ cup) caster (superfine) sugar

60 g (2¼ oz) unsalted butter, melted

1 egg

125 g (4½ oz/1 cup) self-raising flour

40 g (1½ oz/⅓ cup) unsweetened cocoa powder

125 g (4½ oz/1¾ cup) dark mint-flavoured chocolate, roughly chopped (see Note)

230 g (8 oz/1 cup) soft brown sugar

ice cream, to serve

1 **Preheat the oven** to 180°C (350°F/Gas 4). Grease a 1.5 litre (52 fl oz/6 cup) capacity ovenproof dish.

2 **Whisk together the milk,** sugar, butter and egg in a bowl. Sift the flour and half the cocoa powder onto the milk mixture, add the chocolate and stir to mix well. Pour the mixture into the dish. Put the brown sugar and remaining cocoa powder into a bowl and stir in 250 ml (9 fl oz/1 cup) boiling water. Carefully pour this over the pudding mixture.

3 **Bake pudding for** 40–45 minutes, or until it is cooked and is firm to the touch. Spoon over the sauce and serve hot or warm with ice cream.

Note: If you prefer, substitute plain dark chocolate or another type of flavoured chocolate (such as orange chocolate) for the mint chocolate.

PRUNE AND ALMOND CLAFOUTIS

SERVES 6

250 ml (9 fl oz/1 cup) pouring cream

100 ml (3½ fl oz) milk

1 teaspoon natural vanilla extract

3 eggs

80 g (2¾ oz/⅓ cup) caster (superfine) sugar

80 g (2¾ oz/¾ cup) ground almonds

340 g (12 oz) pitted prunes

icing (confectioners') sugar, for dusting

custard or crème anglaise, to serve (see page 51)

whipped cream, to serve (optional)

1 **Preheat the oven** to 180°C (350°F/Gas 4). Lightly grease a shallow 750 ml (26 fl oz/3 cup) capacity ovenproof dish.

2 **Combine the cream,** milk and vanilla in a saucepan. Bring to a simmer over low heat, then remove from the heat and cool slightly.

3 **Whisk together the eggs,** sugar and ground almonds in a bowl. Add the cream mixture and stir to combine well. Scatter the prunes over the prepared dish. Pour the batter over the prunes and bake for 35–40 minutes, or until golden. Dust with icing sugar, pour over the custard and serve with whipped cream, if desired.

MAPLE SYRUP RICE PUDDINGS

SERVES 6

110 g (3¾ oz/½ cup) short-grain rice

750 ml (26 fl oz/3 cups) milk

115 g (4 oz/½ cup) caster (superfine) sugar

1 teaspoon natural vanilla extract

125 ml (4 fl oz/½ cup) thick (double/heavy) cream

60 ml (2 fl oz/¼ cup) maple syrup

115 g (4 oz/½ cup) firmly packed soft brown sugar

pouring cream, to serve (optional)

1 Preheat the oven to 180°C (350°F/Gas 4). Lightly grease six 125 ml (4 fl oz/½ cup) pudding or dariole moulds with butter.

2 Combine the rice, milk, sugar and vanilla in a large saucepan and stir to mix well. Bring to the boil, then reduce the heat to low and simmer for 25–30 minutes, stirring often, or until the rice is tender. Remove from the heat, stir in the cream and set aside for 10 minutes.

3 Spoon 2 teaspoons of maple syrup and 1 tablespoon of the brown sugar into each mould. Top with the rice mixture and bake for 30 minutes, or until set and golden. Rest in the moulds for 15 minutes, then turn out onto plates and serve with cream, if desired.

STICKY DATE PUDDINGS

SERVES 6

185 g (6½ oz/1 cup) pitted dates, roughly chopped

1 teaspoon bicarbonate of soda (baking soda)

70 g (2½ oz) unsalted butter, softened

150 g (5½ oz/⅔ cup) soft brown sugar

1 teaspoon natural vanilla extract

2 eggs

150 g (5½ oz/1¼ cups) self-raising flour, sifted

100 g (3½ oz/1 cup) walnut halves, roughly chopped

CARAMEL SAUCE

155 g (5½ oz/⅔ cup) soft brown sugar

60 g (2¼ oz) unsalted butter

250 ml (9 fl oz/1 cup) thick (double/heavy) cream

1   Preheat the oven to 180°C (350°F/Gas 4). Brush six 250 ml (9 fl oz/1 cup) ramekins with melted butter and line the bases with rounds of baking paper. Put the dates, bicarbonate of soda and 250 ml (9 fl oz/1 cup) of water in a saucepan, bring to the boil, then remove from the heat and leave to cool (the mixture will become foamy).

2   Using electric beaters, beat the butter, sugar and vanilla until light and creamy.

3   Add 1 egg, beat well, then fold in 1 tablespoon of the flour. Add the remaining egg and repeat the process. Fold in the remaining flour, walnuts and date mixture, and mix well. Spoon the mixture into the ramekins.

4   Arrange the ramekins in a large roasting tin, then pour enough hot water into the tin to come halfway up the sides of the ramekins. Cover with foil. Bake for about 35 minutes, or until slightly risen and firm to the touch.

5   To make the caramel sauce, combine the brown sugar, butter and cream in a saucepan over low heat and simmer for 5 minutes, or until the sugar has dissolved.

6   Loosen the side of each pudding with a small knife, turn out onto serving plates and remove the baking paper. Pour the sauce over the top and serve.

CITRUS DELICIOUS

SERVES 4–6

60 g (2¼ oz) unsalted butter, softened

170 g (6 oz/¾ cup) caster (superfine) sugar

3 eggs, separated

125 ml (4 fl oz/½ cup) citrus juice (see Note)

250 ml (9 fl oz/1 cup) milk

60 g (2¼ oz/½ cup) self-raising flour

2 tablespoons finely grated citrus zest

ice cream, to serve

1   Preheat the oven to 180°C (350°F/Gas 4). Grease a 1.25 litre (44 fl oz/5 cup) capacity ovenproof dish.

2   Cream the butter and sugar in a bowl using electric beaters until pale and fluffy. Add the egg yolks one at a time, beating well after each addition. Stir in the citrus juice, milk, flour and zest, combining well.

3   Whisk the egg whites in a clean, dry bowl until stiff peaks form, then gently fold into the batter. Spoon the mixture into the dish. Put the dish in a large roasting tin and pour in enough hot water to come halfway up the side of the dish. Bake for 40–45 minutes, or until golden and puffed (cover the dish with foil if the top starts to brown too quickly). Serve hot or warm with ice cream.

Note: Use a combination of oranges, lemons and limes for the juice and zest.

STEAMED GINGER PUDDING

SERVES 8

60 g (2¼ oz/½ cup) plain (all-purpose) flour

185 g (6½ oz/1½ cups) self-raising flour

2 teaspoons ground ginger

1 teaspoon mixed spice

½ teaspoon ground cinnamon

125 g (4½ oz) unsalted butter, cut into cubes

125 ml (4 fl oz/½ cup) golden or maple syrup

3 tablespoons treacle or molasses

2 eggs, lightly whisked

75 g (2½ oz/⅓ cup) glacé ginger, chopped

custard, to serve

1 **Lightly grease** a 1.5 litre (52 fl oz/6 cup) capacity heatproof pudding basin with melted butter. Line the base with a round of baking paper. Brush a large sheet of foil with butter. Lay a sheet of baking paper on top, creating a pleat in the centre.

2 **Sift the flours,** ground ginger, mixed spice, and cinnamon into a large bowl and make a well in the centre. Place the butter, golden syrup, and treacle in a saucepan and stir over medium–low heat until the butter has melted and is well combined. Allow to cool slightly. Pour the mixture into the flour well, along with the eggs and chopped ginger. Stir until well combined, but do not over-beat as the pudding will become tough.

3 **Pour the mixture** into the prepared basin, cover with the foil and paper, paper side down. Tie securely with string under the lip of the basin. Place the basin on a trivet in a large deep saucepan. Carefully pour boiling water into the pan down the side of the basin to come halfway up the side of the basin, and bring to the boil over high heat. Reduce the heat to medium–low, cover with a lid and simmer for 2 hours, or until a skewer inserted in the centre comes out clean. Add more boiling water to the pan when necessary.

4 **Remove the pudding** from the pan. Allow to stand for 5 minutes before turning out onto a serving plate. Cut into slices and serve with custard.

BREAD AND BUTTER PUDDING

SERVES 4–6

30 g (1 oz) butter, softened

8 slices white bread

2 tablespoons caster (superfine) sugar

2 teaspoons mixed spice

90 g (3¼ oz/½ cup) pitted dried dates, chopped

3 eggs

2 tablespoons caster (superfine) sugar, extra

1 teaspoon grated lemon zest

250 ml (9 fl oz/1 cup) pouring cream, plus extra to serve

250 ml (9 fl oz/1 cup) milk

80 g (2¾ oz/¼ cup) apricot jam

1 **Lightly grease a** shallow baking dish. Lightly butter the bread and cut each slice into four triangles, leaving the crusts on. Combine the caster sugar and mixed spice in a small bowl.

2 **Arrange half** the bread triangles over the dish, sprinkling with all the chopped dates and half the combined sugar and mixed spice. Arrange the remaining bread over the top and sprinkle over the remaining sugar mixture.

3 **Preheat the oven** to 180°C (350°F/Gas 4). Put a baking tin in the oven and half-fill it with hot water.

4 **In a large bowl,** whisk together the eggs, extra sugar and lemon zest. Put the cream and milk in a small saucepan and bring slowly to the boil. Immediately whisk into the egg mixture, then pour over the bread slices. Set aside for about 20 minutes to allow the bread to absorb the liquid.

5 **Cover the pudding loosely** with foil. Bake in the water bath for 15 minutes. Remove the foil and bake for a further 15 minutes, or until golden brown.

6 **Warm the jam** in a microwave or in a small saucepan. Use a pastry brush to coat the top of the pudding with the jam. Return to the oven for 5 minutes. Serve with the extra pouring cream.

RICOTTA AND CREAM CHEESE PUDDING

SERVES 6–8

250 g (9 oz) cream cheese

125 g (4½ oz) fresh ricotta cheese

115 g (4 oz/½ cup) caster (superfine) sugar

125 ml (4 fl oz/½ cup) thick (double/heavy) cream

1 tablespoon warm honey

1 teaspoon natural vanilla extract

5 eggs, separated

30 g (1 oz/¼ cup) sultanas (golden raisins)

35 g (1¼ oz/¼ cup) chopped toasted pistachios

grated zest and juice from 1 lemon

fresh berries and pouring cream, to serve

1 Preheat the oven to 180°C (350°F/Gas 4). Grease a 2 litre (70 fl oz/8 cup) capacity ovenproof dish.

2 Combine the cream cheese, ricotta and sugar in a large bowl and beat with electric beaters until smooth. Add cream, honey and vanilla and beat well. Add the egg yolks one at a time, beating well after each addition. Stir in the sultanas, nuts, lemon zest and juice.

3 Whisk the egg whites in a clean, dry bowl until stiff peaks form, then gently fold into the pudding mixture. Pour into the prepared dish. Put the dish in a large roasting tin and pour in enough hot water to come halfway up the side of the dish. Cover the roasting tin with baking paper, then cover with foil, tightly folding the foil around the edges of the tin to seal. Bake for about 50 minutes, or until the pudding has set and is puffed and firm. Serve with fresh berries and cream.

SPICED QUINCE CHARLOTTE

SERVES 4–6

460 g (1 lb/2 cups) caster (superfine) sugar

1 vanilla bean

1 cinnamon stick

1 teaspoon ground allspice

1.5 kg (3 lb 5 oz) quinces, peeled, quartered and cored

unsalted butter

2 loaves thinly sliced brioche (see Note)

crème anglaise, to serve (see page 51)

1 **Preheat the oven** to 180°C (350°F/Gas 4).

2 **Combine** 1 litre (35 fl oz/4 cups) water and the sugar in a saucepan and stir over medium heat until the sugar dissolves. Split the vanilla bean down the middle and scrape out the seeds. Put the bean and its seeds in the saucepan with the cinnamon and allspice. Remove from the heat.

3 **Place the quinces** in a roasting tin or baking dish and pour over the syrup. Cover with foil and bake for 2 hours, or until the fruit is very tender. Drain the quinces.

4 **Butter the slices of brioche.** Cut out a circle from two slices of brioche (cut a half-circle from each slice), large enough to fit the base of a 2 litre (70 fl oz/8 cup) capacity charlotte mould or ovenproof bowl. Reserving 4 slices of brioche for the top, cut the remaining brioche into 2 cm (¾ inch) wide fingers, and long enough to fit the height of the mould. Press the brioche vertically around the side of the dish, overlapping the strips slightly.

5 **Put the quinces** in the brioche-lined mould and cover with the reserved slices of brioche. Sit the mould on a baking tray and bake for 25–30 minutes. Allow to cool for 10 minutes, then unmould onto a serving plate. Serve with crème anglaise.

Note: Brioche is a rich, sweet, buttery bread that has an almost cake-like texture. It is available from most bakeries. If preferred, substitute with 1 loaf of sliced white bread (crusts removed).

INDIVIDUAL PANETTONE PUDDINGS

MAKES 8

200 ml (7 fl oz) milk

200 ml (7 fl oz) pouring cream

1 teaspoon natural vanilla extract

3 eggs

115 g (4 oz/½ cup) caster (superfine) sugar

150 g (5½ oz) panettone (see Notes)

60 g (2¼ oz/½ cup) sultanas (golden raisins)

custard or crème anglaise (see page 51), to serve

1 **Preheat the oven** to 150°C (300°F/Gas 2). Grease eight 125 ml (4 fl oz/½ cup) timbale moulds with butter.

2 **Combine the milk,** cream and vanilla in a saucepan, heat until almost boiling, then remove from the heat. Whisk the eggs and sugar in a bowl until pale and thick, then gradually add the cream mixture, whisking to combine well.

3 **Cut the panettone** into 1.5 cm (⅛ inch) thick slices and then cut into rounds using a 5 cm (2 inch) cutter (you will need 16 rounds in total). Place a round in the base of each mould, sprinkle over the sultanas, then pour 60 ml (2 fl oz/¼ cup) of the custard mixture over each. Top with another round and enough custard mixture to cover the panettone and fill the mould.

4 **Put the puddings** in a large roasting tin and pour in enough hot water to come halfway up the sides of the moulds. Bake for 25–30 minutes, or until golden and firm. Remove the moulds from the hot water and allow to cool for 5 minutes before inverting onto serving plates. Serve with the custard.

Notes: Panettone is an Italian bread containing raisins and candied citrus peel. It is traditionally served at Christmas and New Year. You could make these puddings using brioche instead of panettone.

GREAT TASTES DESSERTS

SEMOLINA PUDDING WITH SAFFRON APRICOTS

SERVES 8–10

1 litre (35 fl oz/4 cups) milk

230 g (8 oz/1 cup) caster (superfine) sugar

1 cinnamon stick

1 vanilla bean or 1 teaspoon natural vanilla extract

125 g (4½ oz/1 cup) semolina

50 g (1¾ oz) unsalted butter, cubed

5 eggs, separated

250 ml (9 fl oz/1 cup) orange juice

80 g (2¾ oz/⅓ cup) caster (superfine) sugar, extra

1 star anise

a pinch of saffron threads

200 g (7 oz) dried apricot halves

1 Preheat the oven to 180°C (350°F/Gas 4). Grease a 2 litre (70 fl oz/8 cup) capacity ovenproof dish.

2 Combine the milk, sugar and cinnamon stick in a large saucepan. If using the vanilla bean, split it down the middle and scrape out the seeds, then add the bean and its seeds to the pan. Stir over medium heat until the sugar has dissolved; do not allow to boil. Gradually sprinkle the semolina over the hot milk mixture, then, stirring continuously, bring to a simmer and cook for 8–10 minutes, or until the mixture has thickened. Remove from the heat and discard the cinnamon and vanilla bean. Stir in the butter (and the vanilla extract, if using). Remove about 130 g (4½ oz/½ cup) of the semolina mixture to a bowl, add the egg yolks and whisk together. Return the egg and semolina mixture to the saucepan, stirring to mix well.

3 Whisk the egg whites in a clean, dry bowl until stiff peaks form, then gently fold into the semolina mixture. Pour the mixture into the prepared dish. Put the pudding in a large roasting tin and pour in enough hot water to come halfway up the side of the dish. Bake for about 55 minutes, or until the pudding is set and golden.

4 Meanwhile, combine the orange juice, extra sugar, star anise, saffron and 125 ml (4 fl oz/½ cup) water in a small saucepan. Bring to the boil, then reduce the heat and simmer for 10 minutes. Add the apricots and continue to simmer over very low heat for a further 10–12 minutes, or until the apricots are soft and tender. Remove from the heat and discard the star anise. Spoon the pudding into serving bowls and serve hot or warm with the apricots.

COUSCOUS AND APRICOT PUDDING

SERVES 6

90 g (3¼ oz/½ cup) dried apricots, chopped

875 ml (30 fl oz/3½ cups) apricot nectar

1 tablespoon grated lemon zest

1 vanilla bean, split, seeds scraped

1 cinnamon stick

¼ teaspoon ground cloves

1 tablespoon lemon juice

185 g (6½ oz/1 cup) couscous

custard, to serve

1 **Grease six** 250 ml (9 fl oz/1 cup) pudding bowls or ovenproof teacups and place a round of baking paper in the bottom of each. Combine the apricots, nectar, lemon zest, vanilla bean and seeds and cinnamon stick in a saucepan over medium heat and bring to the boil. Reduce the heat and simmer for 5 minutes, then remove from the heat and leave for 5 minutes. Strain, reserving the apricots and discarding the vanilla bean and cinnamon stick. Return the nectar to the saucepan and divide the apricots among the pudding bowls.

2 **Add the cloves,** lemon juice and couscous to the reserved apricot nectar. Bring to the boil, then reduce the heat to low and simmer, covered, for 8–10 minutes, or until most of the liquid has been absorbed. The mixture should still be quite wet.

3 **Spoon the couscous** into the pudding bowls, level the top and cover each with a round of foil. Place the bowls in a steamer and cover with a lid. Sit the steamer over a saucepan or wok of boiling water and steam for 30 minutes, checking the water level regularly.

4 **To serve,** turn the puddings out of the bowls and serve hot with custard.

CARROT AND GINGER SYRUP PUDDING

SERVES 6

60 g (2¼ oz) unsalted butter, softened

55 g (2 oz/¼ cup) soft brown sugar

55 g (2 oz/¼ cup) caster
   (superfine) sugar

2 eggs

4 tablespoons milk

80 g (2¾ oz/½ cup) grated carrot

2 tablespoons finely chopped glacé
   ginger

90 g (3¼ oz/¾ cup) self-raising flour

½ teaspoon bicarbonate of soda
   (baking soda)

½ teaspoon mixed spice

2 tablespoons golden syrup or
   maple syrup

cream, ice cream or custard, to serve

1 Press a large piece of baking paper over the base and into the corners of a 20 cm (8 inch) steamer. Pleat the paper up the sides and allow the paper to overlap the top edges. Spray or brush with olive oil.

2 Using electric beaters, beat the butter, brown sugar and caster sugar in a large bowl until thick and creamy, scraping down the sides of the bowl as you go. Beat in the eggs one at a time. Stir in the milk, carrot and ginger, then add the sifted flour, bicarbonate of soda and mixed spice and stir lightly until combined.

3 Pour the mixture into the steamer and cover with a lid. Sit the steamer over a saucepan or wok of boiling water and steam for 30 minutes, or until the pudding is firm in the centre. Lift out and drizzle the golden syrup over the top. Cut into wedges and serve hot or at room temperature with cream, ice cream or custard.

SPICED TROPICAL FRUIT PUDDING

MAKES 2; EACH PUDDING SERVES 10

750 g (1 lb 10 oz) dried mixed fruit

50 g (1¾ oz) dried mangoes, finely chopped

50 g (1¾ oz) dried peaches, finely chopped

50 g (1¾ oz) sun-dried bananas, finely chopped

50 g (1¾ oz) dried figs, finely chopped

110 g (3¾ oz/½ cup) glacé ginger, chopped

1 granny smith apple, peeled and grated

1 tablespoon grated orange zest

1 tablespoon grated lime zest

110 g (3¾ oz/⅔ cup) unsalted macadamia nuts, chopped

250 ml (9 fl oz/1 cup) dark beer

2½ tablespoons dark rum

210 g (7½ oz/1¾ cups) self-raising flour

1 teaspoon freshly grated nutmeg

1½ teaspoons ground cinnamon

1½ teaspoons mixed spice

250 g (9 oz/heaped 3 cups) fresh breadcrumbs

500 g (1 lb 2 oz/2¼ cups) dark brown sugar

250 g (9 oz) butter

4 eggs, lightly beaten

custard, to serve

1 **Put the dried fruit,** glacé ginger, apple, orange and lime zest and nuts in a large ceramic bowl. Pour on the beer and rum, cover with plastic wrap and leave to soak overnight in the refrigerator, stirring once or twice.

2 **Sift the flour** and spices into a large bowl, then stir in the breadcrumbs and sugar.

3 **Melt the butter** in a small saucepan and whisk in the eggs. Stir this into the soaked fruit and fold in the dry ingredients until fully combined.

4 **Grease the base** and sides of two 1.25 litre (44 fl oz/5 cup) pudding basins with melted butter. Place a round of baking paper in the base of the bowls. Put the empty bowls in two large saucepans on a trivet or upturned saucer and pour enough cold water into the saucepan to come halfway up the sides of the bowls. Remove the bowls and put the water on to boil.

5 **Spoon the mixture** into the pudding bowls. Lay a sheet of foil on the work surface and cover with a sheet of baking paper. Make a large pleat in the middle, then grease the paper with melted butter. Place, paper side down, across the top of one of the bowls and tie string securely around the rim of the bowl and over the top to make a handle. The string handle is used to lift the pudding in and out of the pan. Repeat with the second pudding bowl. Gently lower the bowls into the boiling water, reduce to a fast simmer and cover with a tight-fitting lid. Cook for about 4 hours, checking the water every hour and topping up to the original level with boiling water as needed. Test the puddings with a skewer: if it comes out clean the puddings are ready.

6 **Remove the baking paper** and foil. Invert the puddings onto a plate. Serve warm with custard.

GINGER AND GRAPEFRUIT PUDDINGS WITH MASCARPONE

SERVES 6

1 large ruby grapefruit

40 g (1½ oz/⅓ cup) stem ginger in syrup, drained and finely chopped, plus 3 teaspoons syrup

1½ tablespoons golden syrup or dark corn syrup

125 g (4½ oz) unsalted butter, softened

115 g (4 oz/½ cup) caster (superfine) sugar

2 eggs, at room temperature

185 g (6½ oz/1½ cups) self-raising flour

1 teaspoon ground ginger

4 tablespoons milk

MASCARPONE CREAM

125 g (4½ oz/heaped ½ cup) mascarpone cheese

125 ml (4 fl oz/½ cup) pouring cream)

1 tablespoon icing (confectioners') sugar, sifted

1 **Preheat the oven** to 170°C (325°F/Gas 3). Grease six 170 ml (5½ fl oz/⅔ cup) pudding basins (moulds) or ramekins.

2 **Finely grate 2 teaspoons** of zest from the grapefruit. Slice the grapefruit around its circumference, one-third of the way down. Peel the larger piece, removing any white pith, and cut the flesh into six 1 cm (½ inch) slices. Squeeze 3 teaspoons of juice from the remaining grapefruit. Combine the juice, ginger syrup and golden syrup in a bowl. Spoon the mixture into the basins and top with a slice of grapefruit.

3 **Beat the butter and sugar** with electric beaters until pale and smooth. Beat in the eggs, one at a time. Sift in the flour and ground ginger, add the milk, grapefruit zest and chopped ginger and mix well. Divide the mixture among the basins. Cover each basin with foil and put them in a deep roasting tin. Pour in enough boiling water to come halfway up the side of the basins. Cover the roasting tin with foil, sealing the edges well. Bake the puddings for 30–35 minutes, or until set.

4 **To make the mascarpone cream,** combine the ingredients in a bowl until smooth.

5 **To serve,** gently invert the puddings onto serving plates and serve warm with a good dollop of mascarpone cream.

STICKY FIG AND HAZELNUT PUDDINGS

SERVES 6

70 g (2½ oz/½ cup) toasted hazelnuts

150 ml (5 fl oz) fresh orange juice

100 g (3½ oz/½ cup) chopped dried figs,
   plus 6 dried figs, extra, cut horizontally

¼ teaspoon ground ginger

¼ teaspoon ground cinnamon

3 teaspoons finely grated orange zest

½ teaspoon bicarbonate of soda
   (baking soda)

80 g (2¾ oz) butter, softened

115 g (4 oz/½ cup) soft brown sugar

1 egg

90 g (3¼ oz/¾ cup) self-raising flour

2 tablespoons maple syrup

boiling water, for steaming

thick (double/heavy) cream, to serve

1 **Preheat the oven** to 200°C (400°F/Gas 6). Spread the hazelnuts out on a tray and place in the oven for about 10 minutes. Tip the nuts onto a clean tea towel (dish towel) and gently rub to remove the skins. Put the nuts in a food processor and pulse until finely ground. Grease six 250 ml (9 fl oz/1 cup) ramekins or ovenproof teacups and place a square of baking paper in the base of each.

2 **Pour the orange juice** into a saucepan. Bring to the boil over medium heat. Add the chopped figs, ginger, cinnamon and 1 teaspoon of the orange zest. Cook for 1 minute. Remove from the heat and add the bicarbonate of soda (allowing the mixture to froth), then set aside to cool for 10 minutes.

3 **Meanwhile,** combine the butter and sugar in a large bowl and beat with electric beaters until light and fluffy. Add the egg and beat until well combined. Fold in the hazelnuts, and add

the flour in three batches, incorporating each batch well into the mixture before adding the next (the mixture will become stiff). Pour the orange sauce into the pudding mixture and stir well to combine.

4 **Pour the maple syrup** into the base of the ramekins and top with the remaining orange zest. Arrange two of the extra fig halves in the base of each ramekin. Spoon in the pudding mixture until it is three-quarters full, then cover each ramekin securely with a square sheet of foil. Arrange the puddings in the base of a deep roasting tin. Fill the baking tin with enough boiling water to come halfway up the sides of the ramekins, and bake the puddings for 35 minutes, or until cooked. Set the ramekins aside for 5 minutes before inverting onto a plate and serving with cream.

QUEEN OF PUDDINGS

SERVES 6

500 ml (17 fl oz/2 cups) milk

50 g (1¾ oz) unsalted butter

140 g (5 oz/1¾ cups) fresh breadcrumbs

115 g (4 oz/½ cup) caster (superfine) sugar, plus 1 tablespoon extra

finely grated zest from 1 orange

5 eggs, separated

210 g (7½ oz/⅔ cup) orange marmalade

1 teaspoon honey

whipped cream, to serve

1 **Preheat the oven** to 180°C (350°F/Gas 4). Lightly grease a 1.25 litre (44 fl oz/5 cup) rectangular ovenproof dish.

2 **Combine the milk** and butter in a small saucepan and heat over low heat until the butter has melted. Place the breadcrumbs, the extra sugar and the orange zest in a large bowl. Stir in the milk mixture and set aside for 10 minutes.

3 **Lightly whisk the egg yolks,** then stir them into the breadcrumb mixture. Spoon into the prepared dish, then bake for 25–30 minutes, or until firm to touch.

4 **Combine the marmalade** and honey in a saucepan and heat over low heat until melted. Pour evenly over the pudding. Whisk the egg whites in a clean, dry bowl until stiff peaks form. Gradually add the sugar, whisking well, until the mixture is stiff and glossy and the sugar has dissolved. Spoon the meringue evenly over the top of the pudding. Bake for about 15 minutes, or until the meringue is golden.

5 **Serve** the pudding warm with whipped cream.

PUMPKIN, COCONUT AND CARDAMOM STEAMED PUDDINGS

MAKES 6

125 g (4½ oz) unsalted butter, softened

115 g (4 oz/½ cup) caster (superfine) sugar

3 eggs

90 g (3¼ oz/¾ cup) plain (all-purpose) flour

1½ teaspoons ground cardamom

1 teaspoon baking powder

125 g (4½ oz/1 cup) grated pumpkin (winter squash)

40 g (1½ oz/⅔ cup) shredded coconut

ice cream, to serve

1 **Preheat the oven** to 180°C (350°F/Gas 4). Using electric beaters, cream the butter and sugar until light and fluffy. Add the eggs one at a time, beating well after each addition. Gently fold through the sifted flour, cardamom and baking powder. Stir through the pumpkin and coconut.

2 **Grease six** 185 ml (6 fl oz/¾ cup) pudding or dariole moulds with melted butter. Divide pudding mixture between the prepared moulds. Place the puddings in a large baking tin and pour in enough hot water to come halfway up the sides of the moulds. Cover the baking tin with a sheet of baking paper and then foil. Pleat the foil down the centre and fold tightly around the edges of the pan to seal.

3 **Bake the puddings** for about 30 minutes, or until they spring back when lightly touched. Remove from the water bath and leave for 5 minutes. Turn the puddings onto plates and serve hot with ice cream.

MIXED BERRY SPONGE PUDDINGS

SERVES 6

1 tablespoon melted unsalted butter
125 g (4½ oz) unsalted butter, softened
115 g (4 oz/½ cup) caster (superfine) sugar, plus 6 teaspoons extra
2 eggs
165 g (5¾ oz/1⅓ cups) self-raising flour, sifted
60 ml (2 fl oz/¼ cup) milk
200 g (7 oz) mixed berries, fresh or frozen
custard or ice cream, to serve

1 Preheat the oven to 180°C (350°F/Gas 4). Grease six 125 ml (4 fl oz/½ cup) pudding or dariole moulds with melted butter.

2 Cream the butter and sugar in a bowl using electric beaters until pale and fluffy. Add the eggs one at a time, beating well after each addition. Gently fold in the flour alternately with the milk.

3 Divide the berries between the moulds and top each with a teaspoon of the extra caster sugar. Top berries with the pudding mixture, dividing it evenly between the moulds.

4 Put the puddings in a large roasting tin and pour in enough hot water to come halfway up the sides of the moulds. Cover the baking tin with a sheet of baking paper, then cover with foil, pleating two sheets of foil together if necessary. Fold the foil tightly around the edges of the tin to seal it.

5 Bake the puddings for about 35 minutes, or until they spring back when touched. Remove the puddings from the water bath, leave to cool in the moulds for 5 minutes, then run a small knife around the inside of each mould and turn puddings out onto plates. Serve with custard or ice cream.

LIME AND COCONUT RICE PUDDINGS

SERVES 4

200 ml (7 fl oz) milk

800 ml (28 fl oz) coconut cream

1 lime, zest finely grated

60 ml (2 fl oz/¼ cup) lime juice

3 kaffir lime leaves, halved

140 g (5 oz/⅔ cup) medium-grain rice

100 g (3½ oz/¾ cup) palm sugar (jaggery) shaved or 100 g (3½ oz/ ½ cup) soft brown sugar

toasted shredded coconut for decoration (optional)

1 **Put the milk,** coconut cream, lime zest, juice and leaves in a large saucepan and bring to the boil. Add the rice and stir to combine. Reduce the heat to low and simmer, stirring occasionally, for 25–30 minutes, or until the rice is tender.

2 **Remove the saucepan** from the heat and add the palm sugar, stirring until it has dissolved and the mixture is creamy.

3 **Remove the lime leaves** and divide the rice pudding among four 250 ml (9 fl oz/1 cup) capacity heatproof glasses or ramekins. Serve warm or cold, decorated with the toasted shredded coconut, if using.

LIME AND RICOTTA PUDDING

SERVES 4

60 g (2¼ oz) unsalted butter, softened

350 g (12 oz/1½ cups) caster (superfine) sugar

2 teaspoons finely grated lime zest

3 eggs, at room temperature, separated

375 g (13 oz/1½ cups) fresh ricotta cheese or good-quality tub of ricotta

30 g (1 oz/¼ cup) self-raising flour

60 ml (2 fl oz/¼ cup) lime juice

2 teaspoons icing (confectioners') sugar

1 **Preheat the oven** to 180°C (350°F/Gas 4) and grease a 1.5 litre (52 fl oz/6 cup) capacity ovenproof dish.

2 **Using electric beaters,** beat the butter and caster sugar with half the lime zest for 30 seconds, or until combined. Add the egg yolks, one at a time, and beat until well combined. Gradually add the ricotta and flour alternately and beat until the mixture is thick and smooth. Stir in the lime juice.

3 **Beat the egg whites** until stiff peaks form and gently fold into the ricotta mixture in two batches. Pour the mixture into the prepared dish and place in a roasting tin. Pour enough hot water into the tin to come halfway up the sides of the dish. Bake for 1 hour.

4 **Sift the icing sugar** over the warm pudding and sprinkle with the remaining lime zest. Serve warm.

BROWN SUGAR CREAM POTS

SERVES 6

2 eggs, at room temperature

2 egg yolks, at room temperature

250 ml (9 fl oz/1 cup) thick (double/ heavy) cream

1 teaspoon natural vanilla extract

250 ml (9 fl oz/1 cup) milk

165 g (5¾ oz/¾ cup soft brown sugar, firmly packed)

6 plums, halved, stones removed

2 tablespoons dessert wine

1 tablespoon caster (superfine) sugar

1 **Preheat the oven** to 150°C (300°F/Gas 2).

2 **Whisk the eggs**, egg yolks, cream and vanilla in a heatproof bowl until combined. Stir the milk and brown sugar in a small saucepan over low heat until the sugar has dissolved. Heat until almost boiling, then remove from the heat. Add 60 ml (2 fl oz/¼ cup) of the hot milk to the egg mixture and whisk to combine, then whisk in the remaining milk mixture.

3 **Strain the mixture** into a container with a pouring lip. Pour into six 125 ml (4 fl oz/½ cup) ovenproof ramekins. Put the ramekins in a deep roasting tin and pour enough boiling water into the roasting tin to come halfway up the sides of the ramekins. Bake for 45 minutes, or until set. Set aside to cool for 30 minutes.

4 **Meanwhile,** increase the oven to 200°C (400°F/Gas 6). Arrange the plums on a baking tray in a single layer, cut side up. Drizzle with the dessert wine and sprinkle with the caster sugar. Roast for 12 minutes, or until the plums soften and the skin blisters. Cool to room temperature, then serve alongside the cream pots.

BAKED CHOCOLATE PUDDINGS

SERVES 6

1½ tablespoons cocoa powder

120 g (4¼ oz/heaped ¾ cup) good-quality dark chocolate chopped

120 g (4¼ oz) unsalted butter, softened

3 eggs, at room temperature

2 egg yolks, at room temperature

55 g (2 oz/¼ cup) caster (superfine) sugar

90 g (3¼ oz/¾ cup) plain (all-purpose) flour

CHOCOLATE SAUCE

80 g (2¾ oz/½ cup) chopped good-quality dark chocolate

125 ml (4 fl oz/½ cup) thick (double/heavy) cream

1 **Preheat the oven** to 180°C (350°F/Gas 4) and grease six 125 ml (4 fl oz/½ cup) metal dariole moulds. Dust the moulds with the cocoa powder.

2 **Put the chocolate** in a small heatproof bowl over a small saucepan of simmering water, making sure the base of the bowl doesn't touch the water. Allow the chocolate to melt, then add the butter. When the butter has melted, stir to combine, then remove from the heat.

3 **Beat the eggs,** egg yolks and sugar in a large bowl with electric beaters until thick, creamy and pale. Gently fold in the chocolate mixture. Sift in the flour and gently fold through.

4 **Spoon the mixture** into the prepared moulds, leaving about 1 cm (½ inch) at the top of the moulds to allow the puddings to rise. Bake for 10 minutes, or until the tops are firm and risen.

5 **Meanwhile,** to make chocolate sauce, put the chocolate and cream in a small heatproof bowl and melt over a small saucepan of simmering water, making sure the base of the bowl doesn't touch the water. Stir until combined.

6 **To serve,** run a knife around the moulds to loosen the puddings, then carefully turn out onto serving plates. Drizzle with the sauce and serve immediately.

CHOCOLATE AND CINNAMON SELF-SAUCING PUDDINGS

SERVES 4

50 g (1¾ oz/⅓ cup) good-quality dark chocolate, chopped

60 g (2¼ oz) unsalted butter, cubed

2 tablespoons cocoa powder, sifted

160 ml (5¼ fl oz) milk

125 g (4½ oz/1 cup) self-raising flour

115 g (4 oz/½ cup) caster (superfine) sugar

80 g (2¾ oz/⅓ cup firmly packed) soft brown sugar

1 egg, at room temperature, lightly beaten

CINNAMON SAUCE

1½ teaspoons ground cinnamon

50 g (1¾ oz) unsalted butter, cubed

60 g (2¼ oz/⅓ cup) soft brown sugar

30 g (1 oz/¼ cup) cocoa powder, sifted

thick (double/heavy) cream, to serve

1 **Preheat the oven** to 180°C (350°F/Gas 4) and grease four 250 ml (9 fl oz/1 cup) ovenproof dishes.

2 **Combine the chocolate,** butter, cocoa and milk in a saucepan. Stir over low heat until the chocolate has melted. Remove from the heat.

3 **Sift the flour** into a large bowl and stir in the sugars. Add to the chocolate mixture with the egg and mix well. Spoon the mixture into the prepared dishes, put on a baking tray and set aside.

4 **To make the cinnamon sauce,** put 375 ml (13 fl oz/ 1½ cups) of water in a small saucepan. Add the cinnamon, butter, brown sugar and cocoa and stir over low heat until combined.

5 **Pour the sauce** onto the puddings over the back of a spoon. Bake for 40 minutes, or until firm. Turn out the puddings and serve with thick cream.

COCONUT RICE PUDDING WITH SPICED SAFFRON APPLES

SERVES 4

140 g (5 oz/⅔ cup) short-grain rice

250 ml (9 fl oz/1 cup) milk

270 ml (9½ fl oz) light coconut cream

20 g (¾ oz) unsalted butter

2½ tablespoons caster (superfine) sugar

SAFFRON APPLES

3 small red apples

185 ml (6 fl oz/¾ cup) apple juice

1 cinnamon stick

a pinch saffron threads

50 g (1¾ oz/¼ cup) soft brown sugar

1 **Put the rice,** milk, coconut cream and 100 ml (3½ fl oz) of water in a heavy-based saucepan over low–medium heat. Bring to the boil, then reduce the heat and simmer, stirring often to prevent the rice from sticking, for 15–20 minutes, or until the mixture is creamy. Beat in the butter and sugar.

2 **Meanwhile,** to make the saffron apples, halve and core the apples, then cut into slices. Put the sliced apples, apple juice, cinnamon stick, saffron threads and brown sugar in a saucepan over low–medium heat. Bring to the boil, then reduce heat and simmer for 8 minutes, or until apple is soft.

3 **Serve the rice pudding warm,** topped with the saffron apples and their syrup.

DESSERT BASICS

SHORTCRUST PASTRY

Makes 380 g (13½ oz)

200 g (7 oz/1⅔ cups) plain (all-purpose) flour, sifted

120 g (4¼ oz) chilled unsalted butter, chopped

1   If making pastry using a food processor, put the flour, butter and ¼ teaspoon salt in the food processor. Using the pulse button, process until the mixture resembles coarse breadcrumbs. Add 60 ml (2 fl oz/¼ cup) chilled water, adding the water gradually, and pulse just until a dough forms, being careful not to overprocess. If the dough is dry and not coming together, add a little more water, 1 teaspoon at a time. As soon as the mixture comes together, turn it out onto a lightly floured work surface and press into a flat disc. Cover with plastic wrap and refrigerate for 30 minutes.

2   If making the pastry by hand, sift flour and salt into a large bowl. Add the butter. Using your fingertips, rub the butter into the flour until the mixture resembles coarse breadcrumbs. Make a well in the centre. Pour 60 ml (2 fl oz/¼ cup) chilled water into the well, then stir with a flat-bladed knife to incorporate the water. When the mixture starts to come together in small beads of dough, gently gather it together and lift it out onto a lightly floured work surface. Gently press the dough together into a ball, kneading it lightly if necessary until the dough comes together. Press into a flat disc, cover with plastic wrap and refrigerate for 30 minutes. The dough is now ready to use. Roll out the dough and proceed as directed in the recipe.

SWEET SHORTCRUST PASTRY

Makes 400 g (14 oz)

200 g (7 oz/1⅔ cups) plain (all-purpose) flour, sifted

85 g (3 oz/⅔ cup) icing (confectioners') sugar, sifted

100 g (3½ oz) chilled unsalted butter, chopped

1 egg yolk

1   If making pastry using a food processor, put the flour, icing sugar, butter and a pinch of salt in the food processor. Using the pulse button, process until the mixture resembles coarse breadcrumbs. Combine the egg yolk with 1 tablespoon chilled water in a small bowl. Add to the flour mixture and, using the pulse button, process until a dough forms, being careful not to overprocess. If the dough is dry and not coming together, add a little more water, 1 teaspoon at a time. Turn out onto a lightly floured work surface and press the dough into a flat, round disc. Cover with plastic wrap and refrigerate for 30 minutes.

2   If making the pastry by hand, sift the flour, icing sugar and a pinch of salt into a large bowl, then add the butter. Using your fingertips, rub the butter into the flour until the mixture resembles coarse breadcrumbs. Make a well in the centre. Combine the egg yolk with 1 tablespoon chilled water in a small bowl. Pour it into the well, then stir with a flat-bladed knife. When the mixture starts to come together in small beads of dough, gently gather the dough together and lift it out onto a lightly floured work surface. Gently press the dough together into a ball, then press into a flat disc. Cover with plastic wrap and refrigerate for 30 minutes. The dough is now ready to use. Roll out the dough and proceed as directed in the recipe.

Notes: The kitchen needs to be as cool as possible when making pastry. It is really important not to overwork the dough or it will become tough. Butter should be cold, straight from the refrigerator. Cut the butter into even sized pieces, about 5mm (¼ inch) thick. Always used chilled water to bind the dough. Flour should be sifted before use. This will remove any lumps and incorporate air into the flour, helping to make the dough light. Always rest dough in the refrigerator for at least 30 minutes. If the dough is too cold to roll out it will crack easily, so leave at room temperature, still covered in plastic wrap, for 15 minutes to soften. Always roll from the middle outwards (not using a back-and-forth motion) and rotate the pastry frequently as you go to keep the required shape. If the dough feels really soft and starts to stick to the work surface, roll it out between two sheets of baking paper. Shortcrust (and sweet shortcrust) pastry keeps well once made. Cover with plastic wrap and refrigerate for up to 3 days. It also freezes for up to 3 months.

1 **Preheat the oven to 200°C** (400°F/Gas 6). Lightly grease or line a baking tray with baking paper. Put the water, butter and sugar in a small saucepan and heat until the butter has melted and the mixture has just come to the boil. Add the flour and, using a wooden spoon, stir over medium heat until the mixture comes away from the side of the saucepan, forming a ball. Place the mixture in the bowl of an electric mixer fitted with a whisk attachment and allow to cool slightly. Add the eggs one at a time, beating energetically after each addition and making sure that each egg is thoroughly incorporated before adding the next. (Alternatively, you use a hand mixer or wooden spoon to mix the ingredients.) The mixture should be thick and glossy. The pastry is now ready to use. Pipe, spoon or shape it according to the recipe you are using.

2 **To make choux puffs,** place teaspoonfuls of the mixture on lightly oiled baking trays, spacing them 4 cm (1½ inches) apart. Bake for 25 minutes, or until puffed and golden. Turn off the oven. Using a skewer or small, sharp knife, pierce the base or top of each profiterole to release the steam (they will turn soggy, if you don't). Return the profiteroles to the oven, leave the door slightly open, and let them dry out for about 15 minutes. Transfer to a wire rack to cool completely.

3 **To make éclairs,** put the choux pastry into a piping bag fitted with a 2 cm (¾ inch) plain nozzle. Pipe 10 cm (4 inch) lengths of choux onto the baking tray, spacing them 4 cm (1½ inches) apart. Bake as for choux puffs.

For the best results: Always preheat the oven before beginning to make the choux pastry because it is cooked immediately after it is shaped or piped. Add the flour to the boiling mixture in one go. Immediately beat the mixture with a wooden spoon to prevent lumps forming. Stop beating as soon as the soft dough comes away from the side of the pan and remove from the heat. Always allow the hot mixture to cool for 2–3 minutes before adding eggs or they will start to cook. Beat in the eggs one at a time, making sure they are completely incorporated before adding the next egg. Vigorous action is required. The dough should be piped or shaped while it is still warm. Leave 4 cm (1½ inches) between the piped or spooned dough, allowing room for spreading during cooking. Choux pastries will keep, stored in an airtight container, for up to 3 days. To refresh, if necessary, place on a baking tray and heat in a preheated 180°C (350°F/Gas 4) oven for about 8 minutes, or until the pastry is dry and crisp.

CHOUX PASTRY

Makes about 40 choux puffs and 16 éclairs

250 ml (9 fl oz/1 cup) water

100 g (3½ oz) unsalted butter

1 teaspoon caster (superfine) sugar

140 g (5 oz) plain (all-purpose) flour

3 eggs

Lining a tart tin

Carefully fold the pastry back over and around the rolling pin and lift it gently from the work surface.

Unroll over the tin and ease in, pressing to fit the sides. Roll the pin across the top to cut off the excess dough.

Baking blind

Line the tin with baking paper, then pour in baking beads, uncooked rice or dried pulses (eg, chickpeas, lentils).

Cook for 15 minutes at 200°C (400°F). Lift out paper and beads and bake for a further 5 minutes..

INDEX